JUST BECAUSE I'M
BLACK

Book published

Motivational and Inspirational Thoughts for All People: Seven Hundred Thoughts, Comments, and Essays in Most Fields and Aspects of Life

Books to be published

- *The Ten Commandments of God Vs the Ten Commandments of Satan*
- *1000 Revolutionary Thoughts to Revolutionize the World*

JUST BECAUSE I'M
BLACK

SULLY GRAND-JEAN, MPA
Foreword by Nathaniel G. Higgs, PhD

authorHOUSE®

AuthorHouse™ LLC
1663 Liberty Drive
Bloomington, IN 47403
www.authorhouse.com
Phone: 1-800-839-8640

Published by AuthorHouse 04/08/2014

ISBN: 978-1-4918-5116-6 (sc)
ISBN: 978-1-4918-5123-4 (e)

Library of Congress Control Number: 2014903747

Contents

Dedication

This book is dedicated to Jesus of Nazareth, my mother, my wife, and my children; to the first African American president of the United States of America, Barack Obama, and his wife, Michelle; to the U.S. Senate Chaplain Barry Black; to Trayvon Martin's parents and relatives; to Oprah Winfrey, Dr. Bill Cosby, Nelson Mandela, TD Jakes, Dr. Joseph Lowery, Louis Farrakhan, and Desmond Tutu; to Dr. Nathaniel G. Higgs, Dr. Shonda Shaw, Dr. Richard Freeman, Dr. Jean Robert Charles, and Dr. Leslie Francois Manigat; to the NAACP, the black race all over the world who enjoyed the year of 2009 with their new black president; to all those who are seeking for the union of whites and blacks, to those who are still enchained and are thirsty for liberation, to the needed, the little guys, the orphans, and the street children; and especially to the fans of my newly released book, *Motivational and Inspirational Thoughts for All People.*

Foreword

It is a privilege to know the author and to recognize his pursuit of excellent achievement. Not only is he an author, but he is a philosopher, historian, linguist, and theologian. His collection of provocative, intuitive, and poetic sentiments arranged for handy usage is a catalyst for dynamic public speaking on black affairs.

This publication highlights the struggles and experiences of black people in the United States. In focusing upon this history, the author reflects upon the injustices of the past inflicted upon the descendants from Africa. He draws upon the experiences of the past generation to expose a new generation to the reality of yesteryear.

If you find an appreciation for this book, I should invite you to read other publications by Pastor Sully Grand-Jean.

Nathaniel G. Higgs, PhD

Acknowledgment

I thank Jesus for my life and for keeping me healthy and giving me wisdom and love to write this book to better serve humanity.

I also thank my parents and my family for all their support.

I extend my recognition to Dr. Higgs, a retired scholar, for reading and appreciating my first book, and for reviewing and making the foreword of this second book.

I deeply appreciate the significant service of Verlillian Rucker to review and endorse this book.

I have to acknowledge the tremendous effort of Elite Scholars Academy who has modeled the way, by preparing world rounded young scholars to become effective world leaders. We are changing the next generation, one student at a time.

Special recognition goes to my dear friend and colleague, Kyeron Gray, PhD candidate, who reviewed this book as a critical thinker and shared with me her generous feedback.

A special thanks to Mrs. Miyoshi Bourget for her professional review and guidance.

I admire the members of Jerusalem des Ondes Prayer Ministry for their prayers and support, specifically Rose Denis Salomon, Marie Pierre, Ange Eustache, Jolaine Orvil, Margareth Bossous, Edel Mezidor, and Nadege Jean Noel.

Finally, I greatly appreciate the advice of author and pastor Simeon Nerelus, my former student, to separate the "Just Because I'm Black" part from my first book, *Motivational and Inspirational Thoughts*, to make it a distinct book, which is now a reality. Dany Laferrière, first Haitian and first Canadian to be elected as member of the Académie

Francaise, inspired me to go forward. I consider the support of Alonzo Benjamin, engineer Joseph Gerald Andre, Esther Ormil Jean, and the professional counsel of My-Erline Pierre Garcon to make this second dream come true.

Introduction

History of negritude is one of the most considerable movements in world history. What makes it that great is that it is made with the spirit, soul, heart, body, and blood of the blacks.

"Just Because I'm Black" is an outcry of the marginalized minorities against imperialism and neocolonialism, racism and discrimination, bovarism and nepotism, abuse of power and dictatorship, injustice and unfairness, and exploitation and institutionalized corruption.

This book is written to enhance the self-esteem of black people and help them to accept themselves, give them pride and hope, and inspire them to have the courage to forgive the perpetrators of injustice by presenting black history facts. This literature aims to blow the whistle of the negritude movement to alarm the successful black professionals and business people to give a hand to the black teenagers in the street and homeless under the bridges, to make up their life through social reinsertion programs. It is also to promote the philosophy of negritude to sharpen the pride of the blacks, to thrive for excellence everywhere and in everything.

You will surely find in this work some concerned monologues and dialogues between characters to reveal hidden and unpermitted truths that have been sealed for centuries. "You will know the truth, and the truth will set you free." (John 8:32)

This book is a mixture of history, literature, and poetry. It is a treatise on black civilization, black values, and spirituality. It recalls the pain, suffering, and humiliation of the black slaves in America and relates the barbaric cruelty of the racist whites. It invites readers, mostly the black community, to take action—not to counterattack racist whites, but to forgive and unite with the whites to kill racism.

Throughout this book, you will find truths that will lead to change, reformation, and revolution. This book is designed to motivate you to become a silent activist in changing a corrupt society and fighting for liberty. It will challenge you to regain and maintain independence, seek respect for the constitution, and condemn the institutionalized insecurity that governments use to enslave their citizens.

This book also reveals the hidden errors of most religious leaders who are fooling their members and keeping their souls in captivity. It invites those members to double-check their faith to avoid jeopardizing their eternal life. Watch out!

Chapter I

Good News about Black and Human Species' Origins

Did you know this? The birthplace of every human being is Africa.

Scientists who believe in the evolution myth said the father of mankind left Southern Africa to travel to Australia. As the sea level dropped, they walked on foot about six thousand miles in about ten thousand years.

Dr. Spencer Wells, geneticist, said, "By accident or by design, they made a small boat in wood or sticks to cross the ocean." Dr. Wells said that since early school age, he liked Marco Polo. That's why he traveled on all the seven continents of the world in search of people whose DNA match our ancient travelers coming from Africa to China, Russia, Europe, India, Australia, Brazil, etc.

The first Y chromosome is a male from Africa that spread all the other Y chromosomes throughout the globe for generations and generations. Thus, that first Y chromosome was Adam.

"The Middle East," repeated Dr. Wells "was the bridge to cross all over the world."

With as much pride as excitement, the white man introduced himself, "I am an American. My parents are from Northern Europe. My ancestors are from the Middle East." This came to confirm what the Bible said about the origin of the world including mankind. Eden is geographically located in the Middle East. Let us see where in the Middle East exactly the creator planted the garden and formed man from the dust of the ground. Theologians, theorists, and biblical scholars are curious about the location of Eden. Some evolutionist scientists cling to the Arab view that Eden was located in Yemen and that the

1

burial place of Eve was in the city of Jeddah, Saudi Arabia. *Jeddah* means "grandmother," which provides evidence on why the Arabs named their greatest city after Eve, their grandmother. The faith and actions of the Arabs contradict evolutionist theories, because despite the difference in Arabs' faith from Christianity or the Bible, the Arabs believe that they are living at the burial site of their first mother—or, in other words, their mothers' mother. Thus the Arabs' calling their city Jeddah ("grandmother") shows a connection and faith that they did not come from primates, but from one woman who gave birth to them all. Saudi Arabia is not the garden itself, because it was separated by the two cherubim, but it is Eden and is most likely the place where Eve was laid to rest. If Eve was the first grandmother and lived in the area of Saudi Arabia, this means that Eve was not white; God created man using the dust of the ground and then breathed the breath of life into man (Genesis 2:7) The dust of Saudi Arabia is not white, and neither is the dust of the Middle East.

One group of our first African ancestors went to the North, and another went to the South. Their skin was dark (pigmented because of the ultraviolet rays into their skin). If they had access to fish or to vitamin D, they could have slowed the process. Normally clothes absorb the effect of the sun in the skin.

Dr. Wells confirmed through his genetic research, "There were primates only living in Australia. Then humans came. We were stepping back in time."

If evolutionists said we, humans, are from primates but the primates lived in Australia while human life was discovered through DNA in Africa, evolutionists are wrong and they are misleading humanity. "But there were also false prophets among the people, just as there will be false teachers among you. They will secretly introduce destructive heresies, even denying the sovereign Lord who bought them—bringing swift destruction on themselves. Many will follow their depraved conduct and will bring the way of truth into disrepute. In their greed these teachers will exploit you with fabricated stories. Their condemnation has long been hanging over them, and their destruction has not been sleeping." (2 Peter 2:1-3)

Genes passed down to generations through DNA. Chromosomes come in pairs: YX.

The Y chromosome changes from father to sons. How did Dr. Wells proceed to get an accurate result?

He drew several hundred blood samples to seek matching DNA. He stored DNA in a freezer. While taking the blood of volunteers who decided to participate in the research, he also took their names and their pictures to identify each person to see who made the history.

"All the nations come from a single DNA of a single man coming from Africa," said Dr. Wells.

The DNA of that single man from Africa constitutes the source of human biological paternity. This was Adam, the first man on earth. He was from Africa.

Then, our first travelers went from the Middle East to India to continue their exploration. It took them ten thousand years to continue the documentary. However, the time was not accurate; scientists used a rough estimate to explain the journey of the first travelers. Those who were on their way to Europe designed and painted ceilings of caves that were very tall. In order to reach those ceilings, they had to be very tall too.

They made their way through the Mediterranean. In the process of a long journey and climate change, their skin color, the shape of their noses, and their hair changed gradually.

Dr. Spencer Wells explained his mission: "I travel like Marco Polo to sample the blood of the human descendants."

Amazingly, Dr. Wells found a man in Central Asia whose Y chromosome matched someone else's chromosome in Indonesia.

DNA evidence shows that humanity—blacks and whites, tribes or civilized nations—is one family belonging to our one grandfather and grandmother, Adam and Eve.

It was five thousand miles from Central Asia to America. Going four hundred miles north, there was no heat or electricity at that time. It was sixty degrees below zero in Russia fifteen thousand years ago, and snow covered the ground.

A small group of people left Russia to go fight the cold and loneliness. They moved in the direction of North America. Dr. Wells added,

"Inhabitants had to move because life is a lesson that shows we have to live nearby."

They had to cross the frozen sea that separated Russia from America. The ancient travelers had to make a journey from Africa to the Middle East, from the Middle East to Central Asia, and from Central Asia to North America. Seeking his identity and origin and the origin of the human species, Dr. Wells affirmed again, "In my scientific research I found that we all came from Africa, brothers and sisters, two thousand generations ago."

Rio de Janeiro, Brazil, hosts the most exuberant celebrations of life anywhere on the globe. "My colleague and I have been very lucky to tell this story. The scientific technology simply did not exist. I have been humble. That's why I choose to end my journey here at Rio de Janeiro thirty-five thousand years ago. The ancient travelers left Africa to the New World. I learn a lot. The story carried in our blood is really true. The old-fashioned concept not only divides us but is scientifically wrong."

Again, the estimate of thirty-five thousand years is strongly exaggerated. It is from an evolutionist point of view. Besides, Dr. Wells condemned racism based on his DNA research.

The *World Atlas* reported, "As for Africa, scientists have formerly concluded that it is the birthplace of mankind, as large numbers of human-like fossils (discovered nowhere else) were found in the continent, some dating back 3.5 million years."

This is scientific syncretism, a mixture of truth and error. The truth is, Africa, including the Middle East, is the birthplace of mankind. The error is human-like fossils dated back 3.5 million years.

Dr. Spencer said, "About 1.75 million years ago, early man spread throughout parts of Africa." It is a scientific aberration that earth is billions of years old, just to fit Darwinism. These are few of the biggest lies of history. Let us see what the Bible say about false teachers teaching false doctrines,

"They devote themselves to myths and endless genealogies. Such things promote controversial speculations rather than advancing God's work—which is by faith." (1 Timothy 1:4)

Neither the Carbone 14 nor any more sophisticated archeological instruments give permission to any archeologist to overexaggerate the dating of their artifacts to millions of years. These are idiocies to confuse people and diminish the value of geological science just to please Darwin, with his utopic theory of animalizing mankind.

One day, an archeology student said to her professor, "I just found this rock deep from the ground. Please check to see how old it is."

The professor used the Carbone 14, other instruments, and the lab to date the rock as a discovered artifact. Guess what the professor's answer was. "Wow! You made a scientific discovery! This rock is six hundred thousand years old. It belongs to the Paleolithic period where . . ."

"Okay!" The student smiled and told the truth. "I made this rock myself with cement, water, sand, and clay. Then I formed it into the shape of a knife. When it dried and became a solid, I dug a hole in the ground and buried it. After several months, I dug it up, and you say it's six hundred thousand years old! How come it's older than me if I made it? I'm changing my major!"

Therefore, the one-hundred-thousand-year-old archaeologist dating report is not accurate; millions of years is just a scientific illusion. The same student went to test a geologist science report and made a rock in the shape of a balloon using the same materials. She once again buried it for one full year and dug it back up. When the student brought the rock to the geologist and asked the age of the rock, the geologist, using radiometric, radioisotope, and other dating methods, confidently replied, "One million years old . . ." The student, amused by the geologist's answer, told the geologist the truth, and once again the student defied the report of the geologist, who remained silent.

If there is a Grandjeanism in the future, that will be a theory diametrically opposed to Darwinism; in fact, the so-called "theory" of evolution, or Darwinism, is a nonscientific doctrine that pretends to overthrow God as a creator, steal His copyright, and dehumanize men, who remain the best of creation. If man came from primates or monkeys, why did monkeys stop making human babies? Through evolution, the process should be ongoing! If men came from primates, then that means humans are evolved monkeys. Therefore, men are animals. If men are animals, as there is no salvation for animals and beasts, no man who believes that his origin is from monkeys will go to heaven. "But these people blaspheme in matters they do not understand.

They are like unreasoning animals, creatures of instinct, born only to be caught and destroyed, and like animals they too will perish. They will be paid back with harm for the harm they have done. Their idea of pleasure is to carouse in broad daylight. They are blots and blemishes, reveling in their pleasures while they feast with you. With eyes full of adultery, they never stop sinning; they seduce the unstable; they are experts in greed—an accursed brood!" (2 Peter 2:12-14)

Jesus, creator of the universe, did not die for animals such as primates, but only for human beings who believe that man is a creature of God—only for human beings who believe they come from God and are going to God. The rest will perish with the animals, as they are animals.

There is no Christian evolution or progressive creation; either you are a Christian or a believer of evolution. You cannot mock God. "Those who sit at the gate mock me, and I am the song of the drunkards." (Psalm 69:12). Either you believe in the creation of God—a week of six literal days, with God resting on the seventh day, you come from God through Adam and Eve, and salvation comes from Jesus only—or you believe that the world has been there for billions of years and everything has evolved by means of natural selection. If you believe in the latter, then this satanic influential doctrine above will take you straight to hell.

The Bible explained, "In the beginning God created the heavens and the earth." (Genesis 1:1)

"In the beginning was the Word, and the Word was with God, and the Word was God. He was with God in the beginning. Through him all things were made; without him nothing was made that has been made." (John 1:1-3)

In an article "How We Know the Earth Is Old",
Scientists verified the existence of the oldest man to ever live on earth. "Methuselah," the Bible said. He lived 969 years (Genesis 5:27).

"Some bristlecone pine trees in the White-Inyo mountain range of California date back beyond 2000 BCE. One, labeled 'Methuselah' germinated in 2726 BCE. This is several centuries before the date that conservative Christians assign to Noah's flood. These tree rings have been matched with those of dead trees; this shows that the latter germinated about 6000 BCE, which predates the year 4004 BCE by 2000 years."[1]

Scientists talk about the age of the instruments in iron and in metals. The Bible said Tubal-Cain was the father of instruments in iron and in metals (Genesis 4:22).

As we can see, scientists are just human beings like us, limited in knowledge and ironically in science. They do not possess the whole truth, because the absolute truth belongs to God. Refusing to believe and admit that God created the universe, including the earth, they are looking for other ways to explain creation. Unfortunately, they do not start-off from science to truth, but from lies to science. As the Scriptures said, "And will pay no attention to Jewish myths or to the merely human commands of those who reject the truth." (Titus 1:14) If scientists were looking for the truth about creation, they would have found the truth, agreed, and supported the Bible, but instead they try to prove the lies of evolution scientifically. By intellectual probity, we cannot advocate lies and claim them as truth. That's why they cannot find the truth about creation, and they are using the evolution doctrine of Charles Darwin, Boucher de Crèvecoeur, etc., to try to prove that Darwin is more legitimate than the Bible.9 God created science and gave intelligence to some people to understand science and to explain it to others. Scientists are clueless to what tomorrow may bring. Medical doctors, specialists, brain surgeons, and heart surgeons can't help themselves. They get sick, they suffer from their disease, and they die like any simple man in the street. They can't prevent death, and they cannot reclaim the lives of the dead. Whom will you trust? God, who created science and all knowledge? Or the Scientists who studied the science and the universe that God created?

On the contrary, Dr. Spencer Wells is right to use DNA evidence to prove scientifically that the first Y chromosome comes from the Middle East and that the world relates to the single Y chromosome. He contradicted the evolution doctrine while proving that primates are from Australia and that humans are from the Middle East. There was no geographic relation between primates and humans. He continued to say that humans traveled from the Middle East to Australia and

---

[1]   http://fayfreethinkers.com/tracts/ageoftheearth.shtml

discovered firsthand the primates. How come evolutionist scientists say that humans are from primates? The scientists are wrong unfortunately, and fortunately the Bible is right. As the Bible says, most people will abandon the truth and adopt fables. They prefer lies over truth, and they choose to mock God!

The Bible speaks clearly, while the language of scientists is complex.

Chapter II

Just Because I'm Black

Just because I'm black,
You don't like me.
I don't make myself dark.
You drowned me in the sea
Just because I'm black.

I can't understand
Why you hate me;
When I love you greatly,
You show me no pity.
I don't know where you stand.
In the morning, I served you tea,
But in return, I got whipped like a Dutch horse.
Your hatred gets every day worse.
You keep beating me with a car jack
Just because I'm black.

You are rose, a light pink,
And you make me call you white.
I obeyed, but that's not what I think,
But for you, that's right.
If you were really white,
By too much pride
You would have killed me
To whiten your race, as you started in Germany.
You would not let alive one black person on this earth,

But you are not and you still want to do it.
For you are a maniac;
You are mean to me
Just because I'm black.

You don't like black people,
But you do like the black color don't you?
You wear black suits for your sumptuous occasions.
You drive a high-class black Cadillac, black Hummer,
Black BMW, black Mercedes Benz, and a black Ferrari
With much pride,
And you want to make me believe
My color is derisive!
I am proud to be black.
Are you jealous of me
Just because I'm black?

Be envious of God, who thought of my color
As diversity of nature.
He gave me a pure heart to love,
A humble spirit to deal with everybody,
A bright mind to invent, create, and discover,
A sincere soul to worship God,
A strong body with courage for my self-defense,
And a high-class sumptuous color of skin covering my flesh
To protect me from skin cancer.
This is why I love my creator so much.
I am proud of Him,
And I'm proud of me.
I didn't make myself.
He made me
To please Himself,
Just because I'm black.

Don't be upset and spiteful of me,
Making me pay for something that I did not do.

I am black, that's a blessing!
I don't want to be pink.
My God likes me like this.
I don't need your perms.
I'm proud of my natural hair.
I don't want to buy your skin lotions and products
To lighten my skin.
You're making money off me,
And you're degrading me as a person.
You disregard my culture.
You despise my self-esteem,
And you treat me worse than a wild beast.
You do all of that
Just because I'm black,
But you forget, my white brother.
You came from blacks.

Chapter III

Pharaohs (2000-650 BC)

I am the black Pharaoh
Of the black Egypt.

You are jealous because I was a super gifted genius
Who invented math, medicine,
Philosophy, geometry, trigonometry,
Biology, physiology,
Mummification, pyramids,
Political science, astrology,
Diplomacy, history, etc.
I dominated the world for hundreds of years,
And you were at my feet,
Admiring my greatness.
I was a mystery.
You got mad and jealous.
You killed your human brothers
Just because they are black.
You deny that I came up with the inventions,
And you taught my children that you did.
You stole my patents.
You robbed me
Of my invention rights.
You stole my libraries.
You learned from my own books,
And you screamed, "Eureka! I got it!"
But you got nothing.

You discovered nothing
But what you read from my books,
And you give yourself the credit
Just because I'm black.

By jealousy and hatred,
You took my grandchildren.
You made them understand
That their history just started,
As if they are extraterrestrial,
With no origin,
When you know the history.
You taught them that their history started with slavery
And finished in slavery,
When you know it's bluff.
Black history started in Eden,
Passing by black Pharaohs,
Black supremacy,
Black world empire.
I was your boss, your master,
Your teacher, and your hierarchical superior,
And you told my grandchildren
I was white?

You put my grandchildren in slavery
To avenge yourself
Of my glorious past.
My nose was round like an orange.
My eyes were black like an Ethiopian.
My hair was black and short like a black goat.
My lips were big enough to recognize my race.
My skin was a dark black with no mixture.
My name was Pharaoh, and I shook the world,
And Egypt of Africa was my universal empire,
And that Egypt still exists
With black Egyptians.

Why are you lying to my kids,
Saying, "Pharaoh was white,"
When you know that's not true?
But you said it anyway,
Just because I'm black
Or to destroy the self-esteem of my black children?
So you teach them blacks cannot accomplish that much,
Blacks can't be so successful,
Blacks can't be that great.
Where do you learn that?
From your racist school?
You read it from your racist books,
And you learn it from your racist masters, like Gobineau.
If the school fails,
The teachers are dumb,
So the students are miserable.

You enslaved my great grandchildren.
You seized them
And put chains on their necks,
Their mouth, their hands,
And on their feet,
Separating them from their family
Like detestable animals,
Making me pay for my greatness
And mystery.
You piled them like animals
Or like merchandise
In your boat.
You sold them
To put money in your pocket
And to humiliate them,
Because I'm no longer in power.
You did to them what you could not do to me.
You forced them to work
On your plantations

Far away from home,
Day and night.
You tortured them
To satisfy your anger,
Your jealousy, your racism,
And your hatred,
Just because they are black like me.

You whipped to death
My grandchildren,
Because they are not white like you.
You made women pull chariots instead of horses.
You dismembered the black slaves just to see them suffer,
And you were eating and drinking
Like a professional wicked master.
You just don't care.
They are not human beings
Because they are simply blacks.
Then on Sunday,
You went to your church.
You praise whom, I don't know,
Maybe one of the Egyptian gods.
You presented your tithes
And offerings,
And your pastor was happy with you.
They just don't care.
They're making money off the slaves.
Your slave was the worst beast
On earth.
You burned slaves alive.
You put others alive inside the ground
To satisfy your jealousy.
You stamped them
With hot iron brands,
Like animals, as your private property.
You destroyed my children

Just because they inherited
My greatness.
You did all of that
Just because they were black.

You raped my granddaughters,
And you created a subrace
That you called "mulattoes" or Métis
To divide my own race.
The mulatto forgot about
His black mom
To claim his white father.
So you divided to reign.
You are bad, very bad,
And I don't know why.
Is it just because they were black
Or because you were jealous that blacks were ruling over you?
But you went too far with your crime.
As a professional criminal,
You forced them to work for nothing,
And you sold their children as your private property.
They are not children like yours,
Because they are simply black.
They have no rights
For being black.

You hanged some for no reason
Just because they claimed their freedom.
Just because they were black, seeking liberty.
You disseminated my children
In the so-called "New World."
You drowned some in the Mississippi River.
You make them a generation of martyrs
Just because they are black.

When they could not take it anymore,

They fought for their freedom,
They broke the slavery chain,
And they were free at last.
In some places like Haiti,
That was a complete freedom,
Because they formed a valiant troop
And attacked the wicked.
They won the war
Against Napoleon Bonaparte, first of the whites,
Because the wicked are weak.
My title, first of the blacks,
Was passed to Toussaint L'Ouverture,
Who defeated Napoleon Bonaparte.
But other places,
They still had to fight.
They did not use weapons.
They didn't fight that hard.
They fought with their will
With their strong minds
To get what they needed.
But you never finished giving them their rights,
To give them all their rights.
You think you're right
Because you are white,
And they are wrong
Just because they are black.

You subdivide my race:
"White Hispanics," "African Americans," and "blacks."
You dare to rename the Hispanic mulattoes "white"
To give them racial promotion,
And you change your name
To Caucasian
For your own social promotion,
Because you always want to be
At the top.

You gave them social endorsement
To keep the blacks divided forever.
They accepted it,
And they think they are really white
Because their masters said so.
Mulattoes are 50 percent black and 50 percent white.
How could you jump to 100 percent white?
Where do you drop the 50 percent black?
So I could pick it up.
I don't leave my treasure in garbage.
The blood of the black, although red,
Is still black.

Mulattoes remember the same master
Who mistreated the black,
Did the same thing to you in the past.
It would be a big humiliation
For that master to call you white.
How come now they do it so easily?
They should have a specific reason:
They want to divide you from your black brothers.
Remember, Métis, you are black,
Not white.
Don't let the old master fool you
To satisfy his personal ambitions,
As usual,
To keep you under his feet
Just because you are black.

They have a second category they call
African American.
They separate them from the blacks,
Because they have a third category they call "blacks."
So the African American is neither white nor black,
According to their
Social contradictions

And racial issues repartitions.
Therefore, they consider
The black Americans
Like illegal immigrants
Lost in a foreign country.

The third category
They called blacks.
Are blacks coming from
All over the world
To prevent them from uniting
With the African American
And vice versa,
Because they don't want
The African American
To welcome the other black brothers
So they won't grow as a social class?
They want them
To remain "minorities."
On the other hand,
They call their class
From all over the world,
Mostly Europe,
To come over, enlarging
Their social class
To exert the white supremacy
Against the so-called black.

Cultural domination is their weapon.
They target the black folks.
Some laws
Told the kids
If your parents are whipping you,
Just call 9-1-1,
And the black kids do.
But the white home training

Is different
From the public education.
Whites whip their kids,
And they submit to or obey their parents.
This is a familial division
They inserted
So parents have no control
Over the kids.
Those people come to put the kids
In jail,
Because the blacks get trapped.

Then they come up with the drugs.
Some white kids sell it to get money,
But some blacks unfortunately
Consume it to get messed up.
So they kill the genius brain
Before it grows up,
Just because they are black.

Some laws say at sixteen,
One is allowed to quit school.
Most black kids quit.
They are in the street,
According to the law.
But if, contrarily, the law said,
One needs to graduate high school
Before quitting school,
At least, they could have had
Their high school diploma.
In any law, there is the reverse side.
Since they open a door,
They know who is going to enter.
Some laws target the minority
Just because they are black.

White folks do crimes,
Black folks do time,
Just because they are black.
Innocent blacks are in jail,
Criminal whites are in the street
To pursue their mission,
Just because they are white.

Black boys who made mistakes as kids
Are treated as criminal adults;
White boys who made the same mistakes
Are sent to see a psychologist.
That's a psychological problem,
Because that's a white boy.
They treat him as a human being.
Is it true?
Yes, it is.

If it is true, is it fair?
No, it is not.
It might be fair to you,
Because the racist mentality has been set
To target the black folks,
Just because they are black.

In some neighborhoods,
If a black passes by,
They call the police.
When a crime is committed,
The first question is,
"Have you seen a black man around?"
Some white folks take advantage and
Commit crimes on blacks.
DNA has been inspired by God
For all good purposes,
Mostly to empty jails

Of innocent blacks.
The first thing lawyers should ask:
"DNA evidence?"
Otherwise, black folks will keep paying for crimes,
For just being black.

I had to go through all of these
Just because I'm black,
But I'm still proud to be black.
I will remain black against your wishes.
Remember, I did nothing to you;
You did all of that to me
Just because I'm black.
Nonetheless, white brother,
You are my long time brother,
Because we are all from the same womb in Africa.

Chapter IV

Jesus Christ: No Beginning and No End

I, Jesus Christ, came as black,
And you did the same thing to me,
Just because I became black.
In reality, I was not black before,
Because I am a spirit with no flesh,
No bones, no skin color.
In order to better accomplish
My mission to save mankind,
I had to be flesh like them.
At that time, blacks and poor were neglected.
I had to identify myself to them,
And I gave a lesson of humility
To human generations.
If I came under black supremacy,
Like at the time of the Pharaohs,
I would make myself white
To support the whites,
But you crucified me
Just because I came as black.

I had to support the humble class,
For humans are just one,
Like nature, with diversity of colors
And variety of species.
I did it like that to please myself.
I do like diversity in unity,

Variety in uniformity,
Multiplicity in singularity,
All in order,
Like the universe, my fingerprint,
That I organized.
Nature accepts its diversity
Like flowers, trees, and plants.
Everything stays united.
Animals, beasts, fish, and birds
Accept their plurality.
According to their species,
They remain united.
White dogs and black dogs
Are friends forever.
White pigs and black pigs
Don't eat each other.
White horses and black horses
Don't fight each other
On racial issues.
All creatures tolerate
And support each other
To conserve their species.
Why do humans refuse to respect
The law of nature?

Universe
Is diverse.
It is universal.
Diversity in unity law
Is well respected;
That's my author's right.
Where there is division,
I'm just not there.
All the stars, asters,
Planets, systems, constellations, satellites,
And galaxies

Observe that law.
They move in order,
As they have been told to.
None have been telescoped
Without my will.

In heaven also
The same law reigns.
I created the angels differently
In order to praise me
They are so many,
Diverse but united,
Except the chief rebel angel, Lucifer/Satan,
Who won one-third for his cause.

Unfortunately, humans oppose to this principle
That governs the universe.
Satan influenced the light skin category
To violate my law, rule, and principle,
And make them hate and destroy
The dark skin category.
So humans separate themselves from
"Unity in diversity."
When one ethnic group
Is living by hatred
And dehumanizing and destroying
The other group,
It is rebelling against God Himself,
And I am not happy at all.
Heaven is a place of unity and love;
Racists have no place there.

Yes, I came down on earth
Among the blacks, the poor, the miserable.
Light-skin Hebrews rejected me
Because I was a dark-skin Hebrew.

They were rich Jews.
I was among the poor Jews.
They humiliated me.
I was too dark to be Messiah,
I was too poor to be their king,
And they crucified me,
Just because I was black and poor.
If I came among them
In a light skin and rich family,
They would have yelled,
"Long live the Messiah, king of Jews."
Because I was born in Bethlehem, Nazareth,
Where the poor dark black Jews live,
They screamed, "Crucify Him, crucify Him."
What did I do?
"You are black and poor,
And you want to reign over us?" They said.
"This man cannot be the Messiah.
Nothing serious can come from Nazareth."
The Pharisees felt disgraced to accept
A poor black Messiah.

Pink-skinned people
From the west
Took the picture of a European actor,
From an exceptional beauty
That I did not have,
Skin that I did not wear,
Eyes that I did not see with,
Nose that I did not smell with,
And offer it to the world
As the body that I used.
Go right now to Bethlehem, in Nazareth.
Look at the people who still live there,
And you will have an idea
About the body that I used

When I was in transition on earth.
I did not let anybody
Realize any kind of picture or painting of me,
Because I want those who worship me
To worship in spirit and in truth—
Not a statue, nor a graven image of me—
And I did not want to divide blacks and whites.
I did want to avoid too much pride from the blacks,
Who would know their savior,
The creator of the universe,
Was black just like them.
And also some whites would have said,
"If God is black, let the blacks worship Him."
These are the reasons
I did not let any form
Of picture from me
To pass from generation
To generation.

However, what I wanted to avoid
Has been done by Satan's agents,
Antichrist, chain of darkness,
Who pretended to have a picture of my face,
When a lady wiped my face
With a handkerchief.

That same Antichrist told people that
They had my whole body picture,
Because they have the linen cloth
That wrapped my body when I died.
Nevertheless, they took a Caucasian crucified body.
They wrapped it with a linen cloth
To convince people
They have proof of my crucifixion.
I don't need my enemy to prove
My existence,

Nor my life in this world.
My two witnesses,
The Old Testament
And the New Testament,
Are enough proof
For those who want to believe.

Even my real picture
Would have been a sin.
So the picture of a nonbeliever
To worship for my picture
Is a greater sin.
That's an abomination,
And the whole earth is following
That error again.
Why?
Just because I became black,
They want to falsify history,
As they falsify Scriptures,
To make them say
What they had never said.
The Bible is a textbook to study and to apply
In order to prepare for
Your exam on earth,
To move to the other world.
The Bible is the map that tells the direction
To travel to Heaven.
It is the orientation system to prepare you
For the new job.
If you skip the Bible,
You will surely miss heaven.

As God, I am neither black nor white.
I want blacks and whites to be united
At the foot of the Cross,
Not to worship the Cross,

But to worship Me,
Not in a statue or graven image,
But in spirit and in truth.
However, I keep the same human body
That I wore when I was on earth,
A tortured black body
With scars in hands, feet, and side,
But with a great glory,
The glory of the kingdom
Of the Most High.
I will return on this earth,
Not like the little Jesus
"Born on the twenty-fifth of December"—
This is again a fake date
Given again by the Antichrist,
The beast, and the false prophet,
But like the king of kings
Coming to exert revenge
On earth to punish my enemies,
And the pretended friends
And fake disciples.
Yes, I will come back,
Not to be arrested,
Humiliated, judged,
Condemned, beaten, tortured,
And crucified again,
But as savior of those who followed my steps,
To destroy this earth
With everything in it.
I am Jesus, king of kings,
Lord of Lords,
The first and the last,
The beginning and the end,
The beginning of the creation
Of God,
The "amen," the faithful,

And true witness,
The Great, I am.
My words are certain and true.
I will establish the kingdom of God
On a new earth,
Because the old earth will roll over
Like a carpet and disappear,
Worse than a big earthquake.
Then they will know that
I am the Great, I am.

You have to obey God, not men.
I, Jesus, am your real master.
You need to divorce
The old masters.
"No one can serve two masters. Either you will hate the one and
    love the other, or you will be devoted to the one and despise the
    other . . ."(Mathew 6:24)
They fool you
Just because you are black.
Voodoo is not the black culture;
It is a satanic religion.
You don't have to practice voodoo
Just because you are black.
Satan gave white magic
To white people
And black magic
To black people
To fool them all.
Avoid secret societies
Like freemasonry
And all kinds of interpellations.
Do not invoke any spirits.
Do not pray to any saints,
Neither "Mother Mary" nor Peter nor any others.
No human is holy.

No human is perfect.
No human is above the sin.
Mary was a regular virgin Jewish girl
Among all the others in Israel.
God had to choose a woman's womb
To become human.
He used Mary's fiancé, Joseph,
As a stepfather.
Their mission is accomplished.
That was a grace to them.
Grace means favor, chance,
Or receiving something
That you don't deserve.
That's why Gabriel said to Mary,
"Thou art highly favoured" (Luke 1:28).
Do not bow down to any men
Or statues
Or graven images.
Address your prayer of faith to the God of Abraham,
In the name of Jesus,
And you shall get an answer.
Heaven is my kingdom that I created—like the Universe—
I, only, have the keys.
I will receive the guests that I invited,
Those who believe me
And keep my commandments (John 14:15; Exodus 20:1-17).

"The Lord said,
The outcry against
Sodom and Gomorrah
Is so great
And their sin so grievous
That I will go down
And see if what they have done
Is as bad as the outcry
That had reached me.

If not, I will know" (Genesis 18:20, 21).
The Lord took the form of men to take a walk
In Sodom and Gomorrah,
To prove to all generations
The lowliness, the depravation,
And the degradation
Of homosexuality.
Before they had gone to bed,
All the men from every part of the city of Sodom,
Both young and old,
Surrounded the house.
They called to Lot,
"Where are the men who came to you tonight?
Bring them out to us
So that we can have sex with them" (Genesis 19:4, 19:5).
And God pronounced His verdict against the immoral cities,
"Then the Lord rained down burning sulfur
On Sodom and Gomorrah
From the Lord out of the heavens.
Thus he overthrew those cities
And the entire plain,
Including all those living
In the cities
And also the vegetation
In the land" (Genesis 19:24, 19:25).
In Leviticus 18,
The lord called those practices
"Unlawful sexual relations."
If anyone makes them lawful and legal,
This person or city
Is fighting against God.
The law of God is clear and simple:
"Do not lie with a man as one lies with a woman;
That is detestable" (Leviticus 18:22).
"Do not have sexual relations
With an animal

And defile yourself with it.
A woman must not present herself to an animal
To have sexual relations with it;
That is a perversion" (Leviticus 18:23).
Gays and lesbians are faithful agents of Satan;
They are there to corrupt and collapse society
By destroying families.
They are persecuting me
As powerful enemies.
Satan is their god, as they are working for him.
Some former white slave owners
Initiated few black slaves
To homosexuality
And bestiality.
Then, those same people spread
Those contagious viruses,
As tourists in the poor countries
Where the sex is cheap.
Blacks, my brothers,
Stay away from those stinky practices.
All homosexuals will share hell with Satan;
Those who practice bestiality
Will have the same punishment
As the beasts.
Watch out!

I am holy, and my kingdom is holy.
No homosexuals will enter heaven's gate
Unless they repent sincerely,
They quit definitely,
And they confess their perversity publicly;
Otherwise, they will burn with their city
For offending, persecuting, and insulting God
With their nasty abomination,
A sin against nature.

Pastors, priests, and other religious leaders
Whosoever follows those practices,
The fire of God will devour him/her
With his/her churches
Unless the church expels him/her
Or the members leave him/her alone
In the church building
With his/her cursed family.
On the other hand,
Some Christian pastors tolerate
Gays and lesbians in their churches
By giving them fake hope and saying,
"We will pray for them.
God is good.
We will be saved by grace.
We can't judge anybody."
Those pastors are hypocrites and charlatans.
They know the word of God,
And they know God does not change,
But they want to use the tithes and offerings of the
Gay and lesbian members,
And they don't care about their salvation.
The fire that consumed Sodom and Gomorrah
Will consume those pastors and their churches.

Besides, alas, some people under Satan's influence
Spread a false news, "Jesus was married"
The Bible does not hide anything,
And this is the unique source of faith and trust.
As God who took the human flesh,
I ate, drank, slept, and felt
Like any regular human.
That's why I felt the whip,
The beating, the torture, the slaps
The spit on my face,
And the nails on my hands

And in my feet.
My mission was greater than having a wife and children.
Therefore, I mastered the feeling toward woman
Through prayer and fasting,
So there would be no confusion.
If I took a woman and made children like any regular man,
The same way the Antichrist of Rome called Mary,
Mother of God, to make people pray and bow down to her,
The same way they would have called that wife,
Wife of God, and my own children
Would have been called
"Children of God" to make people worship them
While those who believe in me must be called
Children of God,
That would be too much confusion.
My children are those who trust in me.
Watch out!
Satan is using some people, even some religious leaders,
To introduce doubt into your mind
To better fool you. Be careful!
Read your Bible every day,
And you will answer them.
"It is written," as I did.

You might hear or watch movies
About Jesus having sexual relations
With His own disciples,
Man with man.
These are again satanic heresies
That some homosexual religious leaders,
Along with some other perverse people,
Said and show to spread that abomination
Among fake Christians and those who are weak.
They are looking for excuses.
They want to show the world
If Jesus did it, so you can do it too.

They are leading people to hell.
This is the end of world time.
Satan and his allies are using all kinds of strategies
To deceive the greatest number.
Do not follow the crowd.
In Noah's time,
Only eight people made it.
If you are pastoring a church
And governments force you, by law,
To marry two men or two women,
You must choose either to obey God to go to heaven,
Or to please men to go to hell.
Jewish authorities ordered Peter and John
Not to teach about Jesus,
But they replied,
"We must obey God rather than human beings" (Acts 5:29).

A new world order
Is taking place,
One world day of worship:
Sunday, the mark of the beast;
One world spirituality:
The worship of the beast and its image;
One world economical system:
Neo-communism;
One world social system:
Colonialism and neo-slavery,
Where free slaves will be controlled like robots;
One world culture:
The dictation and the desire of the government
Or the community leader;
And one world education,
Where teachers will teach immoralities by law.

Barack, my beloved son,
I am the one who put you in this position

To slow a little bit the accomplishment of the prophecy.
Don't let the Europeans use you to do their will.
You are a black man.
They have no interest in you but their own.
Do not speed up the prophecy.
Do not activate the end of the world
By globalization or the new world order.
Instead, go back
To the vicious decisions
That Bush took unilaterally
To precipitate
That new world order.
All decisions concerning the future of the country
Need to be passed by Congress,
To be voted upon by the majority.
This position as
Commander in chief
Of the US government
Is very fragile.
You must be careful.
You may be an apostle of peace,
If you do my will or keep my commandments.
On the other hand,
You can become the beast (Revelation 13:11)
That comes out of the earth,
If you continue the Bush program
With that new world order.
The United States is the beast coming out of the earth.
That's the lamb talking
Like a dragon.
That's the false prophet.
Do not recognize
Any unilateral contract
Bush signed with Benedict XVI
Or previously with John Paul II.
The pope cannot be

Your spiritual adviser,
Because he is not
A Christian himself.
He is the Antichrist of Rome.
No one can represent me on earth
But my two witnesses,
The Old and the New Testament.
The popes are the beast coming out of the sea (Revelation 13:1-10).
The papacy system is the Antichrist of Rome.
Beware of them.
If you want to save your soul,
And the souls of your family that you love so much,
And the souls of that great multitude
Who trust you that much,
Follow neither
The pope's program
Nor the European Union agenda.
Do not participate in freemasonry meetings
Nor other secret society meetings.
You are the US president,
But you will still be Barack
After your first and second mandate.
Do not let anyone take advantage of you.
Never go to nor participate in any secret meeting
From anywhere,
Under water below
Or under the earth beneath.
No back-and-forth friendship or diplomatic visit
Between the Vatican and Washington or vice versa.
I will be with you.
I will support you.
Your life is in my hands.
Don't fear anybody,
And you will have not only my protection on this world
But also eternal life for you and your family.
I am Jesus, the lion of the tribe of Judah,

The first and the last,
The God, creator,
The very holy God.
Somebody will have to deal with the new world order
To accomplish prophecy, but not you.
Let the wicked deal with the wicked, but you,
Follow me step-by-step.
Michelle! Please,
Watch over Barack's soul,
And don't let him sell the souls of the American people
To the dragon or Satan.
I am the one who promised a new world,
Where my children will live forever and ever,
From everlasting to everlasting.

So Satan and his allies also promised a new world order,
Where they will reduce the world to a small
Community of robots
That they will lead and guide according to their will.
Barack, that's a warning!
It's up to you to pay attention.
Judas received his warning too,
But he did it anyway.
One had to betray the son of man,
But he did not have to be Judas.
He accepted to be the betrayer.
Barack, avoid being the American Antichrist,
The beast coming out of the earth.
Somebody needs to be that person
To accomplish what the prophets have said before,
But not you.
The promoter of the globalization or new world order
Will be that second beast coming out of the earth.
Do not accept like Judas to become an evil.
You are a leader, not a follower.
That's why you became president.

Do not follow anybody, any group,
Any agenda, any tutor, but the Bible;
Any leader, but Jesus.
I want black and white to be united,
As it was in the beginning.
A Christian can't be racist.
Either you are a Christian or a racist.
Since the beginning, I made Eve a little darker than Adam
So they can have variety of children to fill up the earth.
I am coming soon, no doubt about it.
See what the Bible say about my upcoming return,

"For we did not follow cleverly devised stories when we told you about the coming of our Lord Jesus Christ in power, but we were eyewitnesses of his majesty." (2 Peter 1:16).

Chapter V

Toussaint L'Ouverture: The First of the Blacks (1743-1803)

My name is Toussaint L'Ouverture.
I was an African Haitian.
My father was born a prince.
My grandfather was a king of Arada.
However, my father has been kidnapped
And sold as a slave to the Europeans.
He was enchained and led to the nigger boat,
Sailing to America.
They dropped him off
At the French colony of Saint-Domingue.
I always remembered
I would have been a king
If my father was not captured.
I always lived as a prince to become one day a king,
Although I was a slave.
For the white man,
I was ugly just because I was black,
And I was so skinny and short
That even little children
Mocked me.
So I did vigorous exercises
To become both a strong man
And a fighter.

I learn to read and write when I was forty years old,
Because the white man made it illegal
For a black man to learn
How to read and write.
Therefore, I violated that law,
Because I knew if I wanted to lead that colony as governor,
To govern whites and blacks,
I needed to have a solid education.
So I pleaded with my godfather,
Pierre Baptiste,
Who was an educated free black man,
To teach me.
He was excited to do that,
But I should keep it a secret.
My dad taught me veterinary medicine.
I treated the horses and other animals
On the plantation of my master, Bayon de Libertad.
Since I knew how to read and write now,
I read all kinds of books about
Medicine, law, administration, leadership, politics,
Diplomacy, military art, religion, etc.
I was so smart that once I read a book,
It stayed in my memory forever, from page to page,
As part of my own knowledge and theory to practice.
When I talked about a book,
I could give you the reference page from my memory.
I also read the book of Abbe Raynal,
Who predicted a black Spartacus
That will come to liberate the black slaves,
And I was convinced that he was talking about me.

I remember I was going to church
With my book of prayer in my hand.
A white man snatched my head with a big stick,
Saying, "Don't you know a nigger should not read and write?
Where are you going with that book?"

And blood flowed over my head, my face, my neck,
And stained my white vest.
I could have beaten him up,
But the time had not arrived.
If I did, I would have been arrested,
Or I could have been killed for beating a white man.
And I would lose my vision to free the slaves
And to govern that colony.
Therefore, I waited until the time of the revolution
To avenge that infraction and insult.
I met him again when the colony was upside down,
In flames, smoke, and blood with the slaves' revolt.
I showed him the old vest with the blood stain and said,
"Do you remember me? Do you remember this vest?"
He remembered me and recognized the vest,
But he asked for a chance.
I opened his stomach with my invincible sword.
I did not give him a chance,
Because white people do all kinds of
Unimaginable cruelty to the blacks,
And they forget about God and mercy.
Then, when the blacks take revenge,
They expect the blacks to remember God,
Forgiveness, grace, and chance.
It is just not fair.

I also learned the languages of the colony,
So I spoke fluently
Creole, French, Spanish, English,
And some African dialects.
I read my newspaper daily
To inform myself about what was going on in the world,
Mostly in France.
The American and French Revolutions
Interested me much.

Then I bought my liberty.
I became a free man.
I practiced all that I read,
All that I learned,
All that I knew,
And all that I heard
That could pushed me forward
To my vision.
First I enrolled in the revolution army
Under the commandment of Biassou.
I became his lieutenant,
And we were fighting for Spain
Against France and England,
Who were fighting against each other
To get Saint-Domingue.
Spain needed me to fight for it,
While England
Was negotiating with me.
France itself was seeking me.
Therefore, Europe was after me.
But I did not let the whites use me
As a black man of genius.
I imposed myself with my conditions, and I told them,
"Whosoever really wants to free all slaves
Will have the help
And support of Toussaint L'Ouverture."
I finally realized that Spain
Did not want to liberate the slaves.
England was struggling;
Only France was forced
To liberate the slaves
Because of too much pressure.
Now I decided to join the French Army,
And the cities that I took from France
When I was fighting for Spain,
I gave them back to France

With my invincible sword,
Guns, weapons,
And military strategy,
Because they knew
Since they had Toussaint
At their side,
They would have success, victory,
Honor, and progress.

They claimed me,
And I presented myself on these terms
So no one would ignore my mission and my vision.
"I am Toussaint L'Ouverture.
My name should not be unknown
To anybody.
When one says, 'Toussaint,'
That name should shake the colony.
I seek vengeance.
I want liberty and equality to reign in Saint-Domingue.
I am working to make it a reality.
Let us be united, brothers,
And let's fight for that same noble cause."

The French Army and government were proud of me.
Spain regretted and was scared.
England wished to have me on their side,
But they were too weak.
It did not take me long to become a
Four-star general of the French Army.
I liberated the slaves,
Not only by military strategy,
But also by diplomacy.
I put France in a situation
Where it had no other choice
But to liberate the slaves.
I deported the French officers, commissioners,

Even the French governor Galbaud,
By high diplomacy,
To become not only the chief general of the army
But also the governor of the colony.
I wrote my own constitution,
The constitution of 1801,
To establish a state of law,
Where whites, Métis, and blacks should live together
As free men and equal citizens.
And I named myself governor general for life,
With the right to name
My own successor.
This was a slap in the face of the white men,
An insult to France,
And a great challenge for Napoleon Bonaparte himself.
I always addressed my diplomatic letters to Napoleon
Like this:
"From the first of the blacks
To the first of the whites,"
But Napoleon felt offended
That a black slave was having diplomatic talks
As an equal to him.
I wanted to give a lesson to humanity
That blacks and whites are equal in everything.

I recruited, trained, equipped,
And educated an army
Of more than one hundred thousand troops
To liberate slaves and establish equality
All over the continent of America.
This was a great ambition.
The United States felt unsecured
And threatened.
I reestablished peace
In Saint-Domingue.
All nations were welcome.

All those who were seeking freedom and equality
Were warmly welcome
In Saint-Domingue
Under my government.
Slaves from Latin America, the Caribbean,
And the United States
Came to get refuge in Saint-Domingue,
And the whites were frightened and shaken
Because they knew any time Toussaint's army
Might invade their country to liberate the slaves
From anywhere in America.
I launched a military expedition against Santo Domingo
With only twenty-five thousand troops.
On January 14, 1802,
In two weeks of battle,
I submitted Santo Domingo, Santiago,
And all the cities of the eastern part
Of the island
In order to liberate the slaves
Against Spain.
No one, nothing, nor any army could resist
Toussaint's army.
On January 28, 1801,
A noble Spanish governor,
Don Garcia,
Bowed down to me and handed me the keys to the city.

The clock of the cathedral resounded,
As if there was a national festival or gala service.
The Spanish Army and the crowd
Bowed down to me like I was a king or emperor,
Along with a Te Deum mass.
This was a solemnly sumptuous mass.
As the new governor of the country,
The bishop himself bowed down before me.
Europeans fired twenty-one cannons of salute

To honor a black man,
And their voices repeated,
"Long live Toussaint,
Long live Toussaint,
Long live Toussaint."
The city shook, and this too was an abundance of honor.
The whites bowed down
To a black man!
I avenged the queen of Haiti, Anacaona.
She was hanged in Santo Domingo by the Spanish governor,
Nicolás de Ovando,
Over three hundred years ago.
I governed the entire island.
I was a grandson of a king.
So I had to become king or governor.
No white man could take it away from me.
I had both diplomatic and commercial relations
With the United States and other countries in the world.
I never trusted the white man,
And they were afraid of me.
I planned to launch war expeditions
On the islands and in the neighboring countries one by one
In order to liberate the slaves
And establish equality.
All slave owners and imperialist nations
Like the United States
Would become petrified.
They planned to establish a coalition against Toussaint.
This meant that all my dreams
Wouldn't come true.
I did not care.
I was prepared.
However, I had to focus also
On the prosperity
Of the former richest colony of France in order
To keep it among the richest countries in the world.

The white men said,
"Under Toussaint's administration,
Saint-Domingue became
Much richer.
Peace was established right after a military campaign;
And you can sense that there was strong leadership
And security in place."
Thousands of tourists came from all over the world
To visit Saint-Domingue and to meet Toussaint.
My dream was to make Saint-Domingue a multination
With exuberant world power.
It happened.
The United States, England, Spain, and France
Would not take the chance
To attack Toussaint.
Therefore, they made a coalition
With Bonaparte,
Because they all had one common enemy to fight:
Toussaint L'Ouverture.
England was recognized at that time as "queen of the seas."
It could have blocked French marines
If it was not allied
With Napoleon.
The United States could have faced them too
For invading the American continent
If there was not a coalition.
Spain could have attacked its enemy,
But it did not.

The expedition arrived
In January, 1802,
With eighty-six war boats,
nearly thirty thousand troops,
And munitions.
Napoleon Bonaparte sent his own brother-in-law,
The general Leclerc,

To lead the expedition.
I used to buy weapons and munitions
From the United States
And other countries.
However, this time, nobody agreed to sell me anything,
Because this war was about white supremacy
Against a black man.
I fought the expedition
As hard as I could
By using weapons, guns, and cannons that I had in reserve.
I ordered my generals to burn cities
That could not defend themselves instead of surrendering.
Burn the plantations in order
To discourage the enemies from all their resources.
Saint-Domingue, Haiti, is a mountainous land;
I took advantage of that to bombard the Europeans
From the mountaintop.
This was done to weaken them and diminish their numbers.
Expert generals of Napoleon's army
Had fallen dead or were wounded.
Leclerc, the general in chief himself, was wounded.
If Napoleon came, he would have been wounded also
Or dead.
The country was filled with fire, flames, smoke,
And dark clouds that covered
Saint-Domingue.

Troops choked from the smoke,
While the surviving troops became infected with diseases.
This became a biological weapon for me to continue
To fight peacefully.
If my exterior and commercial relations had provided me
The weapons and munitions that I really needed
To prepare this war,
I would have destroyed them all.
As I lacked weapons and munitions,

I resisted bravely and valiantly
The expedition during five months,
From January 1802 to May 1802.
All was attributed to hard offense
And counterattacks.
Finally, Leclerc was wounded.
There were less than ten thousand troops.
Almost half of them were sick.
I was asked to sign a treaty of peace
That would recognize Leclerc as the new governor.
I would never accept that proposition
If I did not lack weapons
And munitions.
I hesitated for a while.
Finally, I signed the treaty of peace with Leclerc
And recognized him as the governor
Of a devastated
And ruined plantation.
I gave to Leclerc a volcanic desert
To govern
Instead of the world's richest
French colony
That he came fighting for;
Instead of a treaty of peace,
That was a cessation of fire.

I was planning to restart
At the right moment
To finish them up.

Although I seemed to be an invincible opponent
To my enemies,
Leclerc knew that he could never put his hand on me.
And Napoleon was asking him to deport me to France.
There they would reestablish slavery in the country.
He betrayed me.

The French general Brunet sent me
An invitation and a letter, asking me
For advice and to meet at Gonaïves.
As governor and general in chief,
I hesitated.
I decided to go as a brave general who feared no danger.
Unfortunately, I only had my bodyguards.
When I arrived at the place of the meeting,
The French Army was posted all around to fight one man,
Toussaint L'Ouverture.
I tried to escape, but this time there were too many.
My bodyguards could not help me much
While being faced with an army.
If I had come with at least four hundred troops
In the meeting,
I would have made an opening in the whole French Army.
This is why French commissioners called me L'Ouverture.
It means "the man who made an opening
Wherever he passed."
Yes, they were right.
I always made a safe opening in the British
And Spanish army.
I made openings
Where there were no openings.
I always made openings
Where there was no hope.
However, it would take a miracle from God
To make an opening this time.
My mission was over.
The whole French Army surrounded
The house where they would have the pretend meeting.
I had to surrender to protect
My bodyguards.
They arrested me and told me,
"The first consul, Napoleon, desires to see you.
You are going to France."

I remembered that I had deported thousands
Of French officers.
Now it was my time to be deported.
I replied with as much braveness as pride:
"While overthrowing me,
You have cut off Saint-Domingue,
The tree of liberty of the blacks.
However, it will grow back
Because the roots are deep and so many."
This meant that I represented
The tree of the liberty of the blacks
In Saint-Domingue, Haiti.
Although I was deported,
I have made the history of liberty and equality.
They cannot deport liberty and equality
Out of Saint-Domingue
To reestablish slavery,
Because I had formed leaders
To take over to continue
The war on slavery
And on inequality in order
To keep liberty and equality in Saint-Domingue forever.
I trained powerful generals,
such as Dessalines and Christophe,
Who were even more dangerous than me.

When I got into the ship,
I saw my wife and my children
Had also been arrested the same day.
They separated us,
As they once did to the slaves.
They didn't care about black families,
Because in the European mind,
Blacks were not human beings.
They treated us worse than animals and beasts.
They began to torture me in the ship,

But the captain said,
"Attention! Napoleon wants to see Toussaint alive
Face-to-face."
This was Napoleon's dream.
Toussaint L'Ouverture was
The champion of blacks and whites.
Napoleon thought if he could have made this champion
His prisoner,
He would become the champion of the blacks and whites.
He ignored one thing.
Before I left the country,
I nominated Dessalines
"The champion of the blacks and whites."
Therefore, this title didn't go to Napoleon.

Finally, after a long journey,
The ship had arrived in Paris Port.
The news spread over Paris
That Toussaint L'Ouverture was in town.
The city was shaking,
Like an earthquake.
No one could believe that Toussaint had arrived
With no army to invade Paris.
Napoleon desired deeply to see the legendary Toussaint,
The first of the blacks.
I had to see Napoleon Bonaparte,

A short Caucasian who was not strong enough
To fight a little boy.
I felt like slapping him,
But my hands were chained.
I felt like kicking him,
But my feet were chained.
This man could not have had
A single fight with no swords or weapons with
One of my new recruits.

I said to him,
"Bonaparte, give me back my wife and my children."
He did not answer.
He kept asking me,
"What is the secret to your strength?"
I did not answer either.
He said, "The first of the whites is talking to you."
I replied, "The first of the blacks will not answer."
And he continued, "How do you make people panic?"
I replied, "I saw you panic when you first saw me."
He said again, "Toussaint, how do you make openings
So easily in the armies?"
I replied, "Show some respect to me, Napoleon,
And please call me
'general governor for life.'

Napoleon: "I did not recognize that title!"
Toussaint: "But it is a fact."
Napoleon: "Please,
General Toussaint,
Tell me the secret on how you reconstruct
And rebuilt a country
Right after war so successfully and reestablish
Peace, prosperity, and order."
Toussaint: "That's the value of a black man."
Napoleon: "Which foreign bank
Did you put your money in?"
Toussaint: "I am a black man. I respect myself.
I don't manage to enrich myself.
I don't administer
To impoverish others.
I don't lead to exploit the subjects.
I lead to develop and enrich the country and the citizens."
Napoleon: "Do you have money in Saint-Domingue?"
Toussaint: "My money was a paycheck.
Like every normal citizen,

I had to wait for the next paycheck
For extra personal expenses.
I was not a rich man,
But the country was super rich."
Napoleon: "Are you sure you did not hide
Or treasure
Some billions of dollars in some jars of your private house?"
Toussaint: "I have left billions in the public treasury,
Not in my house."
Napoleon: "Where are they exactly?
And I will let you live."
Toussaint: "They are in the colony of Saint-Domingue."
Napoleon: "Is it in the finance secretary building?"
Toussaint: "Saint-Domingue itself is the great treasure.
You need to know
How to manage it."
Napoleon: "So, where is the treasure?"
Toussaint: "You are the first of the whites,
And you don't understand simple instruction?
It is in the administration of Saint-Domingue."
Napoleon: "How come General Leclerc
Didn't find it?"
Toussaint: "Leclerc did not seek it."
Napoleon: "Leclerc is my brother-in-law.
He's part of my family.
He will not hide anything from me."
Where is the treasure so I can tell Leclerc?"
Toussaint: While saying that, Napoleon started choking me.
My voice was grave and low, but I tried to say,
"The treasure of Saint-Domingue is in the plantations,
Factories, industries, office buildings, and the human resources.
Since I had these, I had a treasure on hand to manage and develop.
You sent Leclerc to destroy that treasure
By an unfair war, a war on skin."
Napoleon: "Tell me the secret to manage
That treasure so Saint-Domingue

Can become again the richest French colony."
Toussaint: "That treasure, as I already told you,
Is gone with the war.
The indigenous army opened fire on most plantations,
Industries, factories,
And office buildings
To discourage their enemies.
Almost twenty thousand French troops were killed.
The rest are sick from the flames
And smoke of the burning plantations."
Napoleon: "Leclerc did not tell me anything like this."
Toussaint: "Did he tell you he himself was severely wounded?"
Napoleon: "Leclerc is wounded? Hey, Pauline, my sister,
Come here to hear this.
Leclerc, your husband, is wounded and sick in Saint-Domingue.
You will have to go now."
Pauline Bonaparte: "Yes, Mr. the First Consul."
Napoleon: "Yes, Toussaint, Leclerc is wounded?"
Toussaint: "He could have died with all your troops
If I did not lack arms and munitions."
Napoleon: "That Toussaint is terrible!"
Toussaint: "Napoleon, if you went to Saint-Domingue yourself,
I would treat you like Leclerc."
Napoleon: "I know, I know, I know. That's why I did not go myself.
They told me you are horrible!
Toussaint, you look like a tiny skinny boy,
And you are that terrible!"
Toussaint: "So you are, Napoleon."
Napoleon: "Please, Toussaint, tell me how to rebuild
Saint-Domingue."
Toussaint: "I am going to reveal to you the secret now,
Not because you are torturing me, but because I want to."
Napoleon: "Yes, please tell me.
I won't choke you anymore."
Toussaint: "Finally, the secret to rebuild Saint-Domingue
Is to send a genius there

Who knows military art,
Leadership management skills,
Along with all the attributes of a good leader:
Medical background, people skills, decision making,
A vision, a dream, charisma, seriousness, honesty, Language skills,
    and legislative skills."
Napoleon: "Wow! For Saint-Domingue!
Where will I find that man?
Even I, Napoleon, don't have all those great qualities and skills.
If I could find one man for each skill,
A total of at least ten to twelve leaders,
I would send them as a counsel of governors to lead
Saint-Domingue."
Toussaint: "You need to find one white man
Who possesses all those above skills and qualities
To send to Saint-Domingue."
Napoleon: "That is impossible!"
Toussaint: "So find a black man."
Napoleon: "If a white does not have all those skills,
I don't have to waste my time
To search among blacks."
Toussaint: "However, you will find several men
Among the black people."
Napoleon: (Napoleon got mad and furious and started shaking
    Toussaint from the neck.)
"Name one black man with all those previous skills and qualities
    without omitting any."
Toussaint: "The one who was leading the colony
Had all of those skills and qualities and many more."
Napoléon: "Say the name."
Toussaint: "Dr. Pierre Francois-Dominique Toussaint L'Ouverture."
Napoleon: "You?"
Toussaint: "Yes."
Napoleon: "What is the secret?"
Toussaint: "The secret is if you cannot find any white man,
Starting with you, your family, your subjects,

Or any white man in France, Europe, or the United States of America,
Send back Toussaint L'Ouverture,
To rebuild the colony in one hundred days."
Napoleon: "How are you going to do that?"
Toussaint: "I've done it many times using the aforementioned skills
    and qualities.
They are mine."
Napoleon: "I will send a white man."
Toussaint: "You sent so many whites, and they couldn't do anything."
Napoleon: "But they always trust a white man.
Even a black man
Might be undercover."
Toussaint, I can't send you back to the colony,
Even though I am convinced that you are the man.
You are a multitalented genius and clever man who could bring
    billions of dollars to France's government.
Nonetheless, we have to safeguard the pride of the white supremacy.
There is one thing I can do for you
Instead of torturing or killing you.
I will keep you undercover to give me advice on all my plans,
    projects, and decisions that I will be taking,
Starting now.
Sound great?"
Toussaint: "Thank you for the great honor,
But it does not sound too great to my ear and my understanding.
I am a black man, not a marionette to be used by the white men.
I am also a French citizen,
Since I was leading the French Army
In the colony.
Why should you be ashamed?
Name me publicly,
As I am a qualified French citizen,
As one of your advisers.
Is it just because I'm black?
Why did you give me French citizenship?
Just to use me!

I, Toussaint L'Ouverture, am too great to serve the white men
As an undercover adviser."
Napoleon: "If you don't accept this,
I can't do anything for you,
Except a death penalty."
Toussaint: "If you want to use my service,
You need to treat me as equal to any other white citizen.
Just announce to your staff and your official journal
That the citizen Toussaint L'Ouverture
Is nominated diplomatic adviser to Napoleon Bonaparte.
He is receiving the same salary, allocations, travel expenses, vacation,
And fees as other white advisers.
Then I will accept.
Treat me as equal to you and to the other whites."
Napoleon: "I am sorry. I can't do that.
You are a black man!"
Toussaint: "Does the color of my skin
Diminish my braveness and my honor?"
Napoleon: "Yes, it does. If you were white with all of those great
    qualities and skills,
You would be the world's number one genius,
And you would shake the world."
Toussaint: "I am, and I did."

Furious, Napoleon slapped me. As I was chained, I could not do
    much. I went one step forward and hit his face with the front of
    my head and broke his nose. Guards took him to prison in Fort
    de Joux. The tropical nigger will make acquaintance with snow,
    hail, ice, and glacial temperatures.

Toussaint: (Before leaving) "Remember that you need twelve highly
    qualified whites, including yourself, to replace a black man,
    Toussaint L'Ouverture, as governor of Saint-Domingue."

They took me to that Fort de Joux.
I was imprisoned just because I was black.

Napoleon locked me up in a cold cell
With no fire to warm up,
Just because I was a great black genius.
I caught pneumonia.
Napoleon slapped me,
Because I recognized that I was the world's greatest genius.
I quaked the world with my military strategy.
Napoleon condemned me to death
With no formal court trial,
Because I did not steal the money of the colony
To share with him.
Napoleon hated me,
Because I refused to let him use my brain as a black man
To lead France, dominate Europe,
And extend his hegemony in the rest of the world.
I knew with my help he would surely succeed,
But I would rather die
Than let the white men humiliate me and my race.

I remembered I was sick and I missed my family so much
That I kept repeating on the morning of April 7, 1803,
"Bonaparte, give me back my wife and my children.
Napoleon, I forgive you because you are my blood brother;
Blacks and whites are originally brothers and sisters,
Although you refuse to admit it."
Then Toussaint died that same day.

Chapter VI

Arthur John (Jack) Johnson (1878-1946)*

I am Jack Johnson.
I won the title of the World Heavyweight Champion
In boxing on December 26, 1908.
I was the first black man to win this title.
I fought racism through boxing.
I knocked out a white man
Named Jim Jeffries,
A former retired champion
Who the racist whites
Brought back to the scene
To knock me out.
Then they started to show respect
To the black men.
When I knocked a white man out,
I knocked out racism,
And I affirmed the validity of the black culture.
I imposed respect and pride for the black race.
Black men, fight racism
The way you can,
As hard as you can,
But I, Jack Johnson, did with my fist.

* Retrieved November 23, 2011from: http://www.famoustexans.
com/jackjohnson.htm

Chapter VII

Emmett Till (1941-1955)

My name is Emmett Till.
I was fourteen years old
When I got killed.
This incident is filled
With tragedy.
Not a comedy,
It is not funny.
It is not a satire
But a true story
Of a young black martyr,
Victim of racism,
Hatred of Ku Klux Klanism.

Two armed white men
Kidnapped me from my bed when I was sleeping
In my room late at night.

They accused me of talking to a white young woman
While I was a nigger, a black man.
That was an insult to the white supremacy.
They accepted no dialogue, no excuses, and no diplomacy.
They hit my head with their gun,
But they were not satisfied.
They tortured me, but they remained unsatisfied.
They attached a huge fan
To my bleeding head

To satisfy their prejudiced hostility
Or animosity.
They led me to their secret place
To calm their anger.
They threw my body in the Mississippi River,
The cemetery that white racists used
To inhume black men,
To cover up their crimes,
To hide the truth.
When a black man is missing
In Mississippi,
Just go to the Mississippi River
With a good diver.
You may find the body
Of somebody.
Remember, I did nothing to you.
You did all of that to me
Just because I was a black boy.

My body was found in that river.
My mom put it in a coffin
And had a public viewing
To let everybody see the cruelty of the racist whites.
You see! You did all of that to me
Just because I was a black boy.
What did I do to you to mistreat me like that?
Just because I was a black boy?
I did not make myself black.
I was born black.
If I had the privilege
To come back to life
On this earth again,
I would be very proud to become black again.
Would you have the courage
To do the same thing to me again?
Just because I'm black?

My case was one example among millions of cases.
Thousands of blacks disappear.
They never find a finger from their body.
Just because the blacks blacken the neighborhood
With their innocent presence,
So the white men have to whiten their neighborhood
By wiping off the blacks.
Oh my God!

Although witnesses testified against the suspects,
A white judge,
With a 100 percent white jury,
Found them not guilty
Just because they were whites.
If they were not guilty,
That meant I was guilty
Just because I was black.
I was guilty
Not only for talking to a white woman
But also for trusting
The two white men.
I was guilty because I did not have a gun
To protect myself from the bloody tigers.
I was guilty for being lynched by two white men
While I should have known there was no justice for a poor black man.
I was guilty because my God did not avoid that
Just to show the world the cruelty of racist whites.
You did all of that to me
Just because you are white.
I did nothing to you
Just because
I was a little black boy.

If, finally, I did not have a strong faith,
You could have made me curse
My God,

Because you forced me to believe
"I'm nothing.
I can't do anything.
I'm wrong for being black."
You are not wrong for being pink,
But you are wrong for showing me
There is something wrong with me
Just because I'm black.

You kidnapped me
Just because I'm black.
You beat me up
Just because I'm black.
You made me cry
Just because I'm black,
But my God wiped my face
Just because I'm black.
You tortured me
Just because I'm black.
You irritated my body
Just because I'm black.
You mistreated me
Just because I'm black,
But you can't cut off my soul
Just because I'm a black Christian.
You continue to persecute me
Just because I'm black.
You will never stop,
As long as I'm black,
And I will stay black forever
Just because I was born black.
You will keep chasing me
Just because I'm black.
My God will protect me
Just because I'm black,
And you will still get jealous

Just because I'm black.
Did you know, my white brother,
You are also black,
Just because you're from black,
Although your skin is pink?
Although your blood is red?
It is black.
My black blood is in your veins.
We are all black
Just because we're black!

From 1955 to 2009,
Fifty-four years
To take the vengeance of a black boy.
Oh my God!
You take fifty-four years
To stop cruelty, abuse, unfairness, injustice,
And mostly racism,
The virus that contaminated the United States of America.
And you do it,
Not too late,
Not too soon,
But at the right time.
A black president is in power now,
Thank God Almighty.
Barack Hussein Obama comes,
Not to create a black supremacy,
But to forgive white folks,
To destroy racism,
And to establish unity among whites and blacks
To move America forward.
And this is my vengeance.
I don't wish
To kill the KKKs.
I forgive them
Because I am a black Christian.

I want them to repent,
To change,
And to join truthfully the union of blacks and whites.

I was assassinated so black men
Can not only talk to a white woman
But also marry any white woman they want
And live in any neighborhood
They desire.
We, both whites and blacks,
Are human beings.
There is no difference.
You can marry the person you like,
Black or white,
According to your heart.
We are children of the same God.
We must live together
As brothers and sisters
To show mutual love and understanding.

After all, I still have the courage to preach love and forgiveness
In spite of all I had suffered
Just because I was a black Christian teen.

Chapter VIII

Martin Luther King Jr. (1929-1968)

My name is Martin Luther King Jr.
I was a black Christian minister
And a civil rights leader.
I preached nonviolence according to the teachings of Christ.
I had a dream,
But it came true.
Blacks and whites put hands on hands
To shoot racism at the mountaintop,
To put the most qualified
Presidential candidate
In the White House because of the content of his character,
Not just because he was a white man.
Therefore, as a black fit this position the best,
He was elected the first
African American
President of the United States of America.
Barack Hussein Obama has made history,
And the world was shaken
And continues to tremble.

God showed me the vision in my last speech in Tennessee.
I saw the inauguration of a black man
As the first African American
President of the United States of America.
Millions and millions of followers and supporters,
Both whites and blacks,

Were screaming,
"Obama! Obama!
Obama! Obama!"
Free at last! Free at last!
Black Americans are free at last!
I saw the tornado of equality
Putting discrimination upside down,
And I saw the thunder of unity
Giving the signal
For whites and blacks to live together
As brothers and sisters.
I saw the lightning of love
Tearing off the hatred from the heart of white racists
To prepare them for change.

I am Martin Luther King Jr.
I am saved by the grace of Jesus.
Jesus is proud of me,
Because I have done his will.
But I am sad that I don't see Malcolm X.
Both of us were ministers.
Both of us were civil rights leaders.
Both of us got shot
For the black cause.
Both of us died
To put racism out of law.
But where is Malcolm X?
I asked Jesus for Malcolm X.
He did not answer.
I asked him again,
Because I would like to see Malcolm X.
Finally He replied.

Jesus: "Those who don't know me,
I don't know them either.
He knew the truth,

That I am Jesus, the God of Abraham,
The unique way for salvation.
No other name or other book,
But Jesus and the Bible,
Can save you.
With too much pride,
Malcolm X refused to accept me as his personal savior,
And he refused to teach his congregation
To believe in me as the unique God,
King of kings, Lord of Lords.
He chose to preach the Koran
Instead of the Bible.
He prefered Elijah Muhammad
Than Jesus Christ.
Therefore, his heart is full of violence and hatred
That he accumulated from his readings and teachings.
I don't have any room for him.
I am sorry to tell you the truth,
Where I put him
Among the nonbelievers.
You can't go there.
The temperature is too hot."
Martin: "Are you talking about
The lake of fire?"
Jesus: "You said it."
Martin: "Wow! A minister?"
Jesus: "He was not my minister;
He was not preaching the truth."
Martin: "Do you want to send me to tell the Muslims
And those of other non-Christian religions, along with the huge crowd
That used to follow me,
That it is really true,
That salvation is
In Jesus Christ only,
Along with the Bible teachings and practices?"
Jesus: "That's a waste of time.

They will not believe you.
They will not accept that you were Martin Luther King,
That you are now saved,
And that Malcolm X is lost.
Furthermore, the place where you are is very holy.
You can't go to a corrupted place like earth,
Where sinners are fighting for their eternal life,
Where nations are fighting like a jungle for their survival.
They have the teaching of Jesus Christ
In the Bible, in some Christian churches, on TV, on the Internet, etc.
They have to make their own choice.
I created human beings through Adam and Eve,
And I put in them the liberty of choice
That I respect.
I can't force anybody to put their trust in me.
That would be unfair.
And human beings would be just like robots;
Satan does that, not me.
That's why I respect the will of the individual.
Those who believe in me—
I will share my kingdom
With them.
Those who refuse,
Satan will share the lake of fire with them.
I am the unique way,
The savior and the judge.
No matter whether someone believes in me or not in this life,
He/she will still have to face me after death
For rewards/salvation
Or for judgment/condemnation.
One better accept Jesus now
Before it is too late
So one won't regret.
If a Christian minister says
Someone may be saved
Without Jesus,

He is a hypocrite.
He might jeopardize his own eternal life
For fooling people
Or for failing to tell the pure truth
As it is,
I will ask him for the blood of the non-Christians.
My word is certain and true.
See what the Bible said about me:
'Then know this, you and all the people of Israel
It is by the name of Jesus Christ of Nazareth,
Whom you crucified
But whom God raised from the dead,
That this man stands before you healed.
He is the stone you builders rejected
Which has become the capstone.
Salvation is found in no one else,
For there is no other name
Under heaven given to men
By which we must be saved.' (Acts 4:10-12)
If one desires to join Christianity,
Do not join a Catholic church;
It is not a true Christian church.
The pope is an Antichrist.
I don't want anybody to run for a lion
And go take refuge in a tiger region.
If one does, on Judgment Day,
One will say,
'. . . But you told us to join a Christian church
And we did!'
I will reply,
'I am sorry. This one was not a Christian church.'"
Martin: "It is really imperative to make a choice for Jesus
While one is still alive on earth."
Jesus: "Yes, it is!"
Martin: "I really regret Malcolm X."
Jesus: "Come on, Martin!

I understand, but this place is a space of happiness.
You have no time to think about lost souls.
If one needs to avoid hell,
He/she needs to do it on earth.
If someone cares about his/her family,
Relatives, friends, coworkers, neighbors, classmates, roommates,
     or inmates,
One needs to do it while living with those people on this earth.
One needs to spread the word of salvation
In Jesus Christ to everybody,
Mostly to the one he/she loves,
The one whom he/she would like to spend
The eternal life with.
After death will be too late.
I can't change the course of history."
Martin: "It is fair!"
Jesus: "What I have done is done!
So was it written, so shall it be done!"

Chapter IX

Malcolm X

My name was Malcolm X.
I was a Muslim minister
And a civil rights leader.
I was a radical man.
I pushed violence with violence;
I counterattacked very hard.
I showed racism to racists,
And I made them feel the hatred back
To taste the bitterness.
White folks are horrible.
Black folks need to be most terrible
To protect their legacy
And survive as a race.
Otherwise, white folks will destroy them all.
I strongly believed in vengeance.
I could not support injustice
Or tolerate threats
Or accept attacks from anybody.
I felt like attacking the enemies before they even attacked me.
Self-defense sometimes
Might be too late.
I am not a Christian.
I don't believe in forgiveness.
You have to pay me back
No matter what,
No matter how,

No matter when.
I will never forget you until I get you back,
To make you pay for what you own.
I can't live with the white men;
I don't trust them.
I am Malcolm X,
But if I were president,
I would take Bush to court
For what he has done
To the country and to the world.
I would have put all the racist whites in slavery
To make them feel the pain
And suffering.
I would have painted the White House black.
I would have had blacks only
In all positions,
From federal to city.
I would have created
A black supremacy,
But my visit to Mecca for Hajj
Has changed my perspective,
Believing and teaching all whites are racists and wicked.
I have seen whites and blacks
Worshipping together as brothers.
I have personally met many whites
Who are very nice and loving people.
However, I am still fighting racism
And violence severely,
Until my fellow brothers get peace.

Also, I took another lesson from history.
I thought the whites were all racists,
Hypocrites, and betrayers.
But if so many whites
Can support Obama,
That means the whites are not all bad.

We still need to fight racist whites
To collapse racism forever,
But not all whites,
Just because they are white.

I was assassinated
Just because I was fighting the violence of the whites
Against the blacks.
Some whites paid a couple black Muslim brothers
From my own congregation
To shoot me,
And they did.
That's sad!
Some blacks sold their black brothers
To white folks for money.
Therefore, I was a victim
Of the racial segregation
Just because I was black.

However, alas, I, Malcolm X, am greatly deceived.
I thought Allah would have taken me
Through his arms
Because I fought
Our dangerous enemies
With as much zeal as fanaticism,
But I don't see Allah.
I saw the judge Jesus.
He told me his name is not Allah.
The God of Abraham,
Along with his son, Jesus,
Is the unique God.
There is nowhere to go
But through Him.
No other name can give you a chance.
No other prophets
Can do anything for you.

What I was ashamed to preach
When I was on earth,
I have no other choice to say it loud
For those who want to hear it.
I am with Elijah Muhammad,
But he can do nothing for himself.
I have wasted my time.
If only I could see Martin Luther King,
I would have asked him to ask Jesus, the God of Abraham,
To give me a second chance,
As He is the God of grace,
But I can't reach out to King,
And I have been told it is too late.
I had to make that decision when I was still on earth.
I love my Muslim brothers even when they killed me.
I would like them to know the truth.
Just believe that Jesus is the God
Of Abraham,
Who created the universe,
With its content,
The earth with Adam and Eve,
Along with nature.
Just believe that God of Abraham
Took the human form, with the name of Jesus,
To die for us to prevent us from burning in hell.
Just believe and get baptized
In the name of Jesus
For the forgiveness of your sins
And to reign with Him above.
Yes, above I hear the cry of joy
And happiness of the true Christians.
Down there, that's the desperate cry
Of those who lived without Christ
And died without Christ.
It seems that we are under the earth.
We are screaming very loud

Under burning fire.
Can you hear our cry?
Can you feel the heat?
At least you would believe.
I can't escape telling you.
Please, just believe.
I love you so much.
Too many people are perishing.
If you don't want to accept Jesus as your personal savior,
Just read the Bible,
Along with the Koran.
You will compare and contrast.
Then you will make a decisive choice.
Just study or read the life and teachings of Jesus Christ,
Along with the life
And teachings of Muhammad
Or any other prophets,
And you will have an idea.
Just study or read the character of the God of Abraham
With any other gods,
And you will understand
Who the true God is.

I remember when I was on earth,
I did go to Martin Luther King.
I asked him to join me to fight back by violence,
But he refused.
He told me he was following Jesus' life and teachings.
I replied, "We are fighting together for the black cause.
Both of us will get shot.
Both of us will die,
But we will not be at the same place."
While saying that,
I thought I would be in Allah's arms
And he would be in hell
For being a Christian.

That's the reverse of what happened.
Unfortunately, he did not argue
With me.
I regret he did not take his time to teach me the Bible
And more about Jesus.
I would not be here,
Suffering that much.
Hell is real,
But not for true Christians.

Chapter X

Muhammad Ali (1942-Present)

My name is Muhammad Ali.
I was born Cassius Clay,
Bearing the name of the abolitionist,
Cassius Marcellus Clay.
When I became a Muslim,
I legally changed my name to
Muhammad Ali.
I fought racism both ways:
Theoretically
And practically.
I am against the racism ideology,
And I fought it with my own wrist
To physically knock it out.

I was the heavyweight champion of the world in 1964.
Then as a true black man,
I took some time off
To visit Africa to meet my ancestors.
I went to the Middle East to learn more about Muslims.
Then I came back
To professional boxing.
I did want to be great,
And I was the greatest.
I was also a charismatic speaker
To attract my crowd of fans.
I refused to go to the Vietnam War,

Because it was unfair and unrealistic.
Thousands and thousands of troops were dead;
Other thousands were
Prisoners of war,
And so many were wounded.
I did have the support of Martin Luther King on this.
As a professional boxer,
I did fight for the black race
To show racist whites
That the black people can excel in anything they want to
And can become the best.
I did all of that just because I'm a black man.
Remember, we are all black, coming from the womb
Of a unique black woman to populate the earth.

Chapter XI

Barack Obama

You opened your mouth,
And you said, "A black man cannot be president,
Especially president of the United States of America.
We will never put a nigger in the White House."
I listened to you wisely,
But I answered you firmly,
"Yes, we can."
You thought I was crazy,
But today you see the truth.
We don't have to paint the walls of the White House black,
But we just have to spread
The black spirit,
Which is love, forgiveness, and change.
That means
We love you in spite of all.
We forgive your cruelty because you were ignorant.
Now, we come to change the outmoded structures
Of the unfair and unjust societies that you established
Up to 2009,
Two hundred thirty-three years since US independence.
You created a legacy
And a supremacy
Of the so-called whites
To dominate, intimidate, dehumanize,
And marginalize.
Time now is up

To throw the expired systems away.
Time to bury discrimination
And to inhume inequality
In the cemetery of equality,
And we will do it
Just because we are black.

We come here to shake the walls of social contradictions
And to drop the roof of division
In order to create one class of American society,
Where citizens and immigrants
Work hand in hand to do the job.

We have lost our identity,
"United" States,
Because some of the classes were not part of the union.
Now, this identity is found.
We are now united.
We are here to clean the mess that the white folks
Have made in Washington for 233 years.
The Big Stick policy is broken.
We are no longer police of the world to chase some nations
And intimidate others
To create more enemies.
We are here to defend ourselves
And offer our friendship to the world.
We are here to rebuild the economy from the inside,
Lend a hand
To underdeveloped countries
To fight hunger, poverty,
Corruption, illiteracy,
Mass killings, kidnappings, dictatorships, human trafficking,
And civil wars with peace.

Georges Washington was the first president
Of the United States of America.

I am the first black president
Of the United States of America.
I am a liberator
And a popular governor,
Like Abraham Lincoln.
I am a strategic leader,
Like John F. Kennedy,
Solving problems without delay
And making the right decision
At the right time.
I have been sent by God
To fulfill the prophecy of Dr. Martin Luther King Jr.
In the holy period of forty years,
I have come so that Martin's dream comes true.
I am a peacemaker and a supporter of the little guys,
Just like Jimmy Carter.
I am promoting change.
We can't come with the very same people
Every four years for 233 years.
We need change,
And change is on its way.
Effective change will be brought
Through a black president,
Just because I'm black.

Before you passed me the power,
You put the country and the world upside down,
As the greatest challenge
For a president,
But we shall overcome
In the name of Jesus.
Just because I'm black,
You left a cigarette lit on both ends for me to smoke,
But I will smoke it through the middle,
Just because I'm a black man.
I did nothing to you.

You did all of that to me
Just because I'm black.

Mulatto: "A Negro is cleaning the White House,
Not a slave.
A Negro is cleaning the White House,
Not a gardener.
A Negro is cleaning the White House,
Not a maid.
A Negro is cleaning the White House,
Not a nurse's aide.
A Negro is cleaning the White House,
Not a manservant.
A Negro is cleaning the White House,
Not a sitter.
A Negro is cleaning the White House,
Not with Pine-Sol and a mop.
A Negro is cleaning the White House,
Not a plumber.
A Negro is cleaning the White House,
Not with broom and dustpan.
A Negro is cleaning the White House,
Not with a rag.
A Negro is cleaning the White House,
Not a caretaker of the lawn.
A Negro is cleaning the White House . . ."

White man: "Is he a state prisoner?"
Mulatto: "Are you crazy?
A Negro is cleaning the White House . . ."
White man: "Is he working for a construction company?"
Mulatto: You're almost there.
He's the CEO/president
Of a reconstruction company."
White man: "Wow! A Negro!"
Mulatto: "Yes, a Negro."

White man: "What services
Does he provide?"
Mulatto: "He cleans up the mess from public administrations,
Promoting human rights,
Interests, and values
To empower individuals, companies,
Cities, states, and the federal government,
Promoting and exerting, applying,
And executing *change* in all aspects of life,
Everywhere and in everything,
Inside and outside,
Here and over there,
In the United States and all over the world."
White man: "Wow! A Negro?"
Mulatto: "Yes, he is.
A Negro is cleaning the White House."
White man: "What kind of cleaning products does he use?"
Mulatto: The White House is so dirty
There are no cleaning products that can shine it."
White man: "Oh! No hope?"
Mulatto: "Great hope!
High hopes!
The Negro is cleaning the White House,
Not with his hands.
The Negro is cleaning the White House
With his brain,
Just because he's black."
White man: "Wow! I would be so proud to be a Negro too!"
Mulatto: "Really?"
White man: "Yes, I wish I were a Negro now."
Mulatto: "However, I am."
White man: "Are you?"
Mulatto: "Yes, I am."
White man: "But you are a mulatto!"
Mulatto: "Yes, mulattoes are Negros too."
White man: "Oh! Okay!

Congratulations!
I'm proud of you."
Mulatto: "Thank you! Praise the Lord!
You too. You are a Negro because the mother of blacks
And whites was a Negro."
White man: "Really!"

Pause

July 4, 1776
January 20, 2009
Two hundred thirty-three years of white supremacy.
Two hundred thirty-three years of white diplomacy.
Two hundred thirty-three years of black marginalization.
Two hundred thirty-three years of white socialization.
Two thousand nine is the transition of power
Between the darkness and the light,
Between sundown and sunrise,
Between obscurantism and renovation,
Between conservatism and change,
Between recession and abundance,
Between war and peace,
Between hatred and love,
Between mediocrity and professionalism,
Between chaos and organization.
Finally, this is a transition
Between white dynasty
And true democracy.
My administration will be a combination of Lincoln's,
Kennedy's, Carter's, and Clinton's administrations.
This is a new beginning,
A new birth.
The struggle is not yet over.
We just set a solid stone of history.

We need to keep building on.
The Audacity of Hope
Came true and will become
"The Hope of Audacity."

Chapter XII

Trayvon Martin

Acrostic

This is a chocking tragedy,
Repeating the slavery system
And the racial discrimination.
You do the crime, and we do the time!
Verdict is partial and unfair.
Officially, a shooter is in liberty,
No peace for society.

Black males are unsafe and unsecured,
Ending up in trauma, heart attacks, and strokes.
No justice for the unarmed black teenagers:
Judge is white! Jury is white! Murderer is white!
And no chance for the black men!
Males are living now in scary movies.
I am not the killer whale in liberty to destroy life,
Nor the murderer who is imprisoned, though free.

Martin died from the bullets of racist whites.
Animosity, discrimination, prejudice, and
Racism take away human brotherhood.
Trayvon's death was a worldwide sorrowfulness.
Injustice to the young black males divides society.
Nonetheless, we must live as brothers, as we are.

I am a black boy, and my name is Trayvon Martin.
I came to earth in 1995, the way I was conceived.
The God of Abraham who designed Adam
Decided my ethnicity, sex, beauty, character, gifts,
Talents, origin, family, and future
Way before I was born.
As retold, everyone said,
With an exceptional smile,
"Trayvon is a handsome black boy,
With a great love for children,
A talented football player,
Smart enough to accomplish both
The American dream and the Christian dream."
Just because I'm black doesn't mean I'm ugly.
Just because I'm black doesn't mean I'm bad.
Just because I'm black doesn't mean I'm dumb.
Just because I'm black doesn't mean I'm wicked.
Just because I'm black doesn't mean I'm a criminal.
Just because I'm black doesn't mean I'm prey to hunt.
Just because I'm black doesn't mean I deserve no protection.
Just because I'm black doesn't mean I'm a poor lamb
Without defense that the wolf can devour with impunity.
I'm a young black male,
So there is no justice for me in my own country.
Therefore, as a young black male in the States,
I am not a human being.

If I were a bird or a dog, I would still be alive today under
The wildlife law that protects animals.
If a white man killed someone else's dog,
He would have gone to jail and faced charges,
But if he killed a young black male, there is no conviction,
Because it's just a black!
My life is nothing for you, just because I'm black,
And you think you are superior to me just because you are pink or
    have light skin.

I did not choose to be black.
My God designed me like that
Just for His great pleasure,
Because He's a God of diversity:
He created a diverse nature,
Diverse animals,
Different species in all creatures.
Human beings are also diverse.
Animals don't fight or kill each other for the color of their skin or
  feathers.
Unfortunately, humans do.
I'm still proud to be black,
Just because I'm black.

I was passing by to go to my father's house.
The only arms that I bore was
My black skin,
My Skittles,
And my Arizona juice can.
You are allergic to my skin.
I would not mind sharing my Skittles with you if you were hungry,
But you were instead hungry for my flesh.
If you were thirsty,
I would be very proud to share my drink with you,
But you were instead thirsty for my blood,
Because I was a black beast to you.
I could have been your little brother;
However, you don't consider a black man as a brother,
Because I don't look like a person to you.
Your hatred increased.
You chased me.
And you attacked me.
You hit me to provoke a fight
In order to shoot me.
When I felt in danger,
I was crying for help,

But in vain.
It seems nobody wanted to hear the cry of a young black male,
Struggling for his life.
I was like a little black bean lost in the midst of a bag of rice,
With no hope of surviving.
I had to pay with my life for my skin;
That was the only crime I committed.
I was black.
I was enjoying life,
Talking to a friend, eating my Skittles,
Drinking my juice,
And getting ready to watch football with my family,
But I had no right to life
Just because I was black.
You become the hero of the white supremacy
For killing a black beast;
And the law will protect you just because you have light skin;
And that same law condemned me just because I was black.
You claimed self-defense,
And the verdict was "not guilty,"
Just because you are close to white.
My blood claimed justice.
My case was cross-examined,
And the verdict said
I was guilty,
Just because I was black.

You are free to kill other black teenagers.
You are legally empowered to destroy the black community,
But I am the criminal for not showing
Enough respect to the white man.
Should I lick his feet to survive?
Even though I begged for my life,
He had no pity on a black man.
If I were still alive with my bullet in my chest,
I would still be wrong.

I would have chains on both my hands and my feet
At the hospital.
Then I would have been sent to jail,
Judged,
Condemned,
And in the final verdict, I would get a life sentence in prison.
This is justice for a black man in America!
In spite of all of that, I would still prefer life in prison, although
    innocent, than losing my life forever.

My parents could have visited me,
Though this is not the life that I would expect,
But it would still be better than death.
So now, how do you feel, my light-skin brother?
Although you don't accept me as your brother,
Just because I'm black,
How do you feel in your heart?
You did all of that to me,
Just because you are white.
I did nothing to you,
Just because I'm black.

Now you are on the street like an innocent man,
Just because you claim to be white.
I am in the grave like a criminal,
Just because I'm black.
Your soul and conscience will bother you,
And you will turn yourself back into police,
And you will tell this time the whole truth,
And you will try to exhume my body to seek
Forgiveness,
But I will still forgive you,
Just because I'm a black Christian.

Black brothers,
No violence, please!

Violence is cured by love and forgiveness,
But you can still seek justice peacefully.

God's final judgment is near
And will be impartial.
None will escape.
Dead and alive will face it.
He knows in advance who is right
And who is wrong.
"Love your enemy,
Do well to those who mistreat you,"
Ordered Jesus,
So I love you in spite of all,
And I forgive you all,
Just because I'm a black Christian.
Did you know our great grandmother Eve
Was a black woman?
How will you feel when you meet Jesus
At Judgment Day,
And you see a black man
Sitting on the throne of heaven?

Trayvon Martin, treasure of his blessed family,
Resource for the community,
Asset for the world, repeated Emmett Till's history.
Young black teen screamed for help with no answer,
Vainly struggled for his life.
Oh just got shot by a young man
Named George Zimmerman.

Martin thought racial discrimination was finished.
And he thought he was going to make it.
Really, it is a shocking fact.
Trayvon got shot lamentably.
Ironically, Martin Luther King got shot to kill racism.
No, racism is not dead; discrimination is still alive.

Chapter XIII

God

And the Lord said unto George Zimmerman, "Where is Trayvon, thy brother?" And Zimmerman said, "This is not my brother. Does he look like me?" (Genesis 4:9).

And the Lord replied, "What hast thou done? The voice of thy brother's blood crieth unto me from the ground" (Genesis 4:10).

"And now art thou cursed from the earth, which hath opened her mouth to receive thy brother's blood from thy hand" (Genesis 4:11).

"When thou tillest the ground, it shall not henceforth yield unto thee her strength; a fugitive and a vagabond shalt thou be in the earth" (Genesis 4:12).

You said as defense, "Maybe that was the Lord's plan to kill Trayvon? My plan was and will still be 'Thou shalt not kill.'"

The heavenly surveillance camera got everything. You will pay seven times more for the blood of that boy now on this earth and then during the final great judgment on Resurrection Day. My kingdom in heaven has no place for those who nourish hatred, prejudice, discrimination, and racism in their heart.

Verily, verily, I said unto you, "Racists, no matter how good their deeds are, will be thrown to the lake of fire and sulfur, where there will be weeping and gnashing of teeth" (Mathew 25:30).

Zimmerman is free because of racial partiality.

I am the one who created Adam and Eve and set the reproductive system in their body so they could fill up the earth through their generations. I do like diversity a lot.

Superiority of man is not in his skin, but in the heart and mind that love God above all and their human brothers like themselves.

Conclusion

The author believes that he has left in the annals of history this book as a second gift presented to the world, where blacks and whites can forgive each other and forget the offenses to reconcile in order to be united.

May this book be a catalyst for change and a pure source of inspiration to break both physical and spiritual chains from everyone who is enslaved, and may this literature serve as a strong booster for liberation all over the world, where humans are suffering injustice and exploitation. This book will motivate and create silent activists, who will break the chains of slavery in Africa and in the world and make human traffickers face justice to stop forever a centuries-old practice.

A new world order is taking place to switch our twenty-first technological century with the Middle Ages. Globalization, or new world order, is a society of new communists who are chasing and destroying the old ones to come up with a neo-communism and impose it on the whole earth for a very short term, as the end of the world is really imminent. Neo-communists will break human intrinsic and extrinsic values. They will force people to believe, submit to, and follow them. That will be a true social corruption and personality disorder. New world order leaders will destroy moral and family values to moralize immoralities.

The author is convinced that this book is also a spiritual guide designed to awaken spirits and press the alarm to announce to the world that its end has arrived. Salvation is personal, but we can still help each other to be aware of the fragility of the time and the strange events that are going on.

The world is ending. Time is up. Time is over. Let's get ready by being intelligent and making the right decision and the smartest choice. Let us apply the desert survival rules and principles to save our souls. Let us be prudent enough to handle our salvation; to double-check the traditions, beliefs, and practices that we have been using to see if there were any mistakes or errors to correct; and to make a U-turn to seek the right way, the truth. This is the beginning of wisdom.

This book may be one of the most controversial books in a period full of controversial ideas, theories, dogmata, and philosophies. It translates change into poetry, truth into poetry, and history into poetry. It is not a simple collection of poems. It is a source of information for black history, a guide to truth, and a motivation for change. It combines history and sociology, literature and poetry, religion and faith, and black civilization and culture.

While this book enhances black values or negritude, it promotes a true reconciliation through forgiveness between whites and blacks and inspires them to take the path of unity.

Just Because I'm Black is a book for blacks and whites to recall the past, to correct the present, and to prepare a better tomorrow, where whites and blacks will live together in the same house. The change is coming.

Furthermore, this literature is also a self-help book to sharpen the curiosity of the believers to seek the truth in the process of salvation, to put the law and the will of God above all human traditions. On the other hand, the nonbelievers and atheists might meet the superior being they were looking for.

Black brothers and sisters, God has given us a noble black skin. We need to prove our noble hearts to match them.

After all, no one knows what the present and next generations will call the author, "philosopher of negritude" or "historian of negritude," "motivational speaker on black affairs," "black activist," "revolutionary philosopher/poet," etc., but for sure he is neither a black panther nor a racist, because he does not have a heart to hate anybody. His heart pumps up blood into his veins and love into his organs, his mind, his spirit, and his soul. He loves his white brothers and sisters, and he does not come to divide blacks and whites, but he is so sensitive to the crying and screaming of the black brothers for help, aid, understanding, listening, protection, guidance, justice, and fairness, and few people seem to hear them. (While saying this, the author's eyes are watery, and his heart hurts.) He wants to shelter those under the bridges, feed the hunger, help the needy, and assist the young black males who seemed disoriented, discouraged, and desperate. He wants to help the street children through social reintegration programs to turn them into future leaders of the world."

The author loves his black brothers and sisters so much that he would rather die so they could live. With the pride of negritude, he would allow his blood to shed to spare theirs. He would sacrifice himself for their success and happiness. But he's just a sinner. His blood is a simple human specimen that can't do too much.

The blood of Abel shed, but had no salvation power

The blood of Prophet Isaiah shed, but could not save his generation.

The blood of Jesus' disciples shed to spread the good news of the kingdom of the Most High, but could not help that much.

The blood of Toussaint L'Ouverture shed to liberate the blacks, but could not give spiritual liberation.

The blood of Jean-Jacques Dessalines shed, but could not save Haiti.

The blood of Abraham Lincoln shed to keep the states united and to liberate the black slaves, but still can't give us happiness.

The blood of Massillon Coicou shed to maintain patriotism in Haiti; unfortunately we are still seeking loyal patriots.

The blood of Mohandas Gandhi shed to liberate India from British colonization, but it could not satisfy the Indians on all points of view.

The blood of John F. Kennedy shed to give equal rights and opportunities to the black Americans and to stop corruption and establish transparency, but the situation got worse.

The blood of Martin Luther King shed to drown racism and discrimination; however, white supremacy rescued them.

Only the blood of Jesus, our black brother, has healing power, restoration, and deliverance through salvation.

Only Jesus' blood is pure enough to wash the sins of humanity away.

Jesus' blood shed to give true hope to those in despair.

Jesus' blood shed to erase our offenses.

Jesus' blood shed to pardon our crimes and iniquities.

Jesus' blood shed on the calvary to take our guilt and to give us a "not guilty" verdict, if only we believed in Him.

Jesus' blood shed to give to his black brothers a better life on this earth and mostly the eternal life in heaven and on the new earth where slavery, colonization, exploitation, injustice, racism, discrimination, diseases, hunger, poverty, misery, and death will end forever.

Jesus' blood shed to give to His white children the forgiveness of sins, and whosoever believes in Him can have eternal life.

Jesus' blood shed to unite blacks and whites from Adam and Eve to the last generation

Jesus' blood shed to provide the power to blacks and whites to live on this earth with mutual love, as members of the same household

Jesus' blood shed to model the way and pave the road to help blacks and whites make a safe transition to our last itinerary, Heaven.

Jesus'blood shed to offer to blacks and whites a free eternal life insurance including a vacation package of one thousand years in Heaven

Finally Jesus' blood shed to offer a free citizenship to blacks and whites in the New Jerusalem city coming down from Heaven to be established on the new earth where we will live together again forever and ever from everlasting to everlasting. (Revelation 20:1-6).

After being victims of all kinds of crimes and injustices, suffering from diseases and other problems and troubles, we can't afford to miss Heaven. Just believe in Jesus as the God creator, and accept Him as your personal savior. He said, "I am the way, the truth, and the life. No one comes to the Father, except through me." John 14:6 He will take us straight to Heaven. See you there.

Bibliography

Anitei, Stefan. "Who Were the Black Pharaohs?" N.p., 29 Jan. 2008. Web. 03 Jan. 2014.

http://news.softpedia.com/news/Who-Were-the-Black-Pharaohs-77437.shtml?

Gillespie, C. Richard. *Papa Toussaint*. San Jose: ToExcel, 1998.

Grand-Jean, Sully. *Motivational and Inspirational Thoughts for All People: Seven Hundred Thoughts, Comments, and Essays in Most Fields and Aspects of Life*. Xlibris, 2008.

Hodge, Bodie. "How Old Is the Earth?" *Answers in Genesis*. 17 May 2007. Web. 01 Jan. 2014.

http://www.answersingenesis.org/articles/2007/05/30/how-old-is-earth?

Holy Bible: New International Version. Grand Rapids, MI: Zondervan Pub. House, 2001.

"How We Know the Earth Is Old." N.p., n.d. Web. 03 Jan. 2014.

http://fayfreethinkers.com/tracts/ageoftheearth.shtml

James, C.L.R., and James Walvin. *The Black Jacobins: Toussaint L'Ouverture and the San Domingo Revolution*. London: Penguin, 2001.

Keishaw, J., J. Beamish, and C. Maltby, "Journey of Man." United States: PBS Home Video, 2003, DVD

King, Martin Luther, and James Melvin. Washington. *A Testament of Hope: The Essential Writings and Speeches of Martin Luther King, Jr.* San Francisco: Harper, 1991.

"MIDDLE EAST." World Atlas. N.p., n.d. Web. 03 Jan. 2014.

http://www.worldatlas.com/webimage/countrys/af.htm

"New Answers Book 2." Chapter 12: What's Wrong with Progressive Creation? N.p., n.d. Web. 03 Jan. 2014.

http://www.answersingenesis.org/articles/nab2/whats-wrong-with-progressive-creation

Rosen, Ruth. *Jewish Doctors Meet the Great Physician.* San Francisco, CA: Purple Pomegranate Productions, 1998.

Sauveur, Myrlande E. *Daily Spiritual Vitamins and Minerals for Your Soul: Feed Your Soul as You Feed Your Body Every Day.* Outskirts, 2013.

Sutton, William Josiah. *Ancient Prophecies about the Dragon, the Beast, and the False Prophet.* Institute of Religious Knowledge, 1999.

Vandeman, George E. *Planet in Rebellion.* Nashville: Southern Pub. Association, 1960.

Welsh, David, and J.E. Spence. *Ending Apartheid.* Harlow, England: Longman/Pearson, 2011.

White, Ellen Gould Harmon. *The Great Controversy.* DeLand, Florida: Laymen for Religious Liberty, 1990.

Recommended televised programs:

3ABN
TBN
The Hall Lindsey Report (Broadcast)
Forerunner777

Appendix: Racial Injustice Statement

We, the undersigned, feel the pain and suffering of black families when they are the victims of racial injustice. We want to be the voice for those without voices and give everyone the opportunity to sign this petition to demand reform of the US justice system, so that it truly promotes "justice for all" and reinforces the punishment for discrimination, racism, nepotism, and partiality.

Who would have believed that, in the twenty-first century, the United States of America, which claims to have the best judiciary system in the world, the promoters of democracy, exercises neither justice nor democracy itself? Our justice system is racist against young black males, and it is partial to nonblack males. We have a system that is uncomfortable with arresting, judging, and convicting the son of a retired magistrate court judge who killed an unarmed teenager. This is legalized corruption, and justice is not being served.

Injustices like this prove that Martin Luther King's work was in vain. His blood was shed for no reason, because racism is rampant in a system where those in power use their power to disseminate injustice. How can there be justice for the young African American males in the United States when racism rules? There are laws that defend and protect animals, but there are no laws that protect young black males from injustice like this. They are persona non grata in their own country. They are unwelcome in their home country and exiled in their own birthplace.

We, the undersigned, stand against the mistreatment of young black males in the United States who are victims of hatred and racism. We, the undersigned, call for reform and justice and demand that the justice system stop its racist practices that are designed to fill its prisons with black males. We, the undersigned, stand together to demand impartiality in judicial proceedings, free of racial prejudice and discrimination, and demand "justice for all."